From the Viewpoint of the Sioux

THE
WOUNDED KNEE
MASSACRE

JAMES H. McGREGOR

THE WOUNDED KNEE MASSACRE
Printed in U.S.A.
Reprinted 1969/Sixth Edition
Reprinted 1972/Seventh Edition
Reprinted 1984/Eighth Edition
Reprinted 1987/Ninth Edition
Reprinted 1991/Tenth Edition
Reprinted 1993/Eleventh Edition
Reprinted 1997/Twelfth Edition
Reprinted 2001/Thirteenth Edition
Reprinted 2005/Fourteenth Edition
Reprinted 2007/Fifteenth Edition
Reprinted 2010/Sixteenth Edition
Reprinted 2015/Seventeenth Edition

Printed by
FENSKE MEDIA CORPORATION
Rapid City, South Dakota

CONTENTS

1. Dewey Beard
2. James Pipe On Head
3. Rough Feather
4. Louise Weasel Bear
5. George Running Hawk
6. Mrs. Mousseau
7. Bertha Kills Close to the Lodge
8. Edward Owl King
9. White Lance
10. John Little Finger
11. Henry Jackson or Harry Kills White Man
12. Alice Dog Arm or Kills Plenty

13. Peter Stands
14. Donald Blue Hair
15. Afraid of the Enemy
16. Mrs. Rough Feather
17. Frank Sits Poor
18. Richard Afraid of Hawk
19. Black Hair
20. Charles Blind Man
21. James High Hawk
22. Dog Chief
23. Charles Blue Arm
24. Annie Iron Lavatta Hakiktawin
25. Nellie Knife

DEDICATION

This little volume is respectfully and reverently dedicated to the Indian mothers, living and dead, who saw the bodies of their little babies pierced by bullets and who suffered the pangs of death from wounds, inflicted by the soldiers of the United States Army, in violation of the very essence of the Treaty of 1868 and of all humanitarian ideals.

PREFACE

At first thought, the average reader would be inclined to think that there is little excuse, at this late date, for writing an account of the Wounded Knee Massacre, but it should be remembered that about the only thing that has been written, is from the pens of white people, who have often been prejudiced writers and made heroes of the soldiers, and blood-thirsty savages of the Indians. The Sioux have said but little and written less, it therefore, becomes in the interest of justice, a duty toward the survivors, to write the story of the Wounded Knee Massacre, from the Red Man's viewpoint.

The survivors were given an opportunity to relate their own stories, in their own language and in the presence of an Indian audience. Two reliable and competent interpreters were present and translated the speeches as they were spoken and a record was made of them by a stenographer.

Their stories form an important part of this book and it will be noted that the survivors tell their stories in a simple, straight forward manner, without any attempt to relate personal deeds of valor of themselves or their relatives. Their earnestness and the absence of malice or desire for retribution, should convince the most skeptical that they were telling the truth as they remembered it.

4

INTRODUCTORY

The Wounded Knee Massacre occurred December 29, 1890, on the Pine Ridge Reservation about seventeen miles from the Agency. It is often referred to, by white people, as the last stand of the Sioux Indians (and while it was not a stand at all as you will see by reading what the participants have to say), and while it may be the last act so far as even a semblance of military resistance goes, it is safe to say it is not the last stand the Sioux will make so far as influence on public events are concerned. So sturdy and well balanced a race as the Sioux will yet rise, when they find themselves, and will take their proper place in the march of progress that our country is making.

Perhaps there is no other race of people so thoroughly misunderstood as the Indians, and though they are natives of our country, many people know as much about the Hottentots of Africa as they do about the North American Indians, especially the Sioux. In order that the reader may understand the people who suffered so severely and so unjustly at the hands of the Government at the Wounded Knee Massacre and other places, it should be of interest to know more about them from a non-prejudiced source and from their own viewpoint.

The Sioux civilization is of a much higher order than even most of the white people, living in an Indian country, realize as there is not much social intercourse between the Reservation Indians and the better class of white people. Race prejudice is, of course, the primary cause of this lack of social mingling, that even the western hospitality has not been able to break down. True there are racial customs that have a tendency to keep them apart. The white people dance for pleasure and recreation, while the Indians dance because of its deep religious significance. White people pray for spiritual blessings and for the forgiveness of sins, while the Indians formerly prayed for material help and power to overcome the enemy. These basically different views are

5

natural causes that keep them apart and the Indians are too proud and not sure enough of the superiority of the white civilization, over their own, to make any overtures for social recognition. The white people, on and adjacent to the Reservations, are content to let the Sioux continue as they are, believing that it is the duty of the Missionaries to assume the responsibility for the Indians' spiritual progress and welfare.

Business transactions furnish about the only contacts that exist now between the white people and the Reservation Indians, as they have separate churches, separate schools, separate fairs, separate dances and separate community centers. A small number of full blood Sioux attend the public schools, where no prejudice or distinction is shown by the officials or the teachers; but the student body is often permeated with prejudice and the Indian students are aware of its existence. There are exceptions to the above statement as here and there are found individuals, usually mixed bloods, who have such outstanding traits of character and a magnetic personality that enables them to forge ahead, and toward these, little if any, prejudice is shown and in fact special honors are often bestowed upon them.

In chastity the early Sioux civilization compared favorably with that of the better class of white people, but close observation and some mingling with the mediocre white people near the Reservations in the frontier days, has had a telling effect on the younger generation of the Sioux.

Politically the Sioux is much in evidence and it is here he can and does cope successfully with his white brother on equal terms, and more often than not to the advantage of the Red man. Indians say that every two years, during the heat of the campaign, both political parties manifest much interest in the Sioux people, and are very solicitous about their welfare, but after the election this interest soon disappears. Regardless of this, many of the Indians are as thoroughly wed to a political party as are the whites. This class, of course, votes the ticket of their choice consistently, but during the campaign do not hesitate to eat beef belonging to the other political party. They are especially loyal to a political official who has been fair and just with the Indians, and no amount of persuasion or beef will disuade them from voting for their friends. Recently an old Indian woman who could not read or speak English, presented herself at the polling place and announced that she came to vote for Senator Norbeck, and on being informed that his name was not on the ballot she disgustedly left the place without voting.

To the white people who are unacquainted with the Sioux and may wish to visit the Reservation, kindly take warning and never judge an Indian's intelligence or standing in the community by his general appearance or actions, since an educated full blood and prominent Indian, in the presence of white strangers may sit on his horse and gaze out into space as though he had no interest in life, while in reality he has studied you and perhaps has a rather accurate idea of your station in life. His keen eye, alert mind, sensitive ear and silent tongue enables him to quickly comprehend new surroundings and this gift is one of the factors that has made the Sioux an excellent hunter and a great soldier.

People who know the Sioux intimately agree that they are superior intellectually and physically to most any other tribe, but to the man on the street they are just Indians. Strange indeed it is that the Army Officers did not sense this superiority when they were first detailed to the Indian country to try to civilize them, and stranger still it is that the Government did not send school teachers rather than powder and bullets. The Missionaries had preceded the soldiers and were making progress, and soon realized that the Sioux had many excellent qualities and high ideals. If the Army Officers could have but realized this fact, history would have a different story to record and the Government would have been saved the chagrin it must often bare for the unfair treatment it accorded its Native Americans. Be it said to the credit of the Army Officers, that later in life they realized the importance of Indian civilization and became true friends of

7

the Indian people and often visited them after their retirement. General Miles and General Scott are noble examples of this class.

First impressions are said to be the most lasting and as the Indians' general knowledge of the white people was gained, largely through their association and observation of the soldiers, they formed erroneous ideas. Many of the Army officials received their first knowledge of the Indians from their experience with the Southwest tribes, and as they are less intelligent than the Sioux and have very different customs, so the Army officials who were later sent north were poorly qualified to deal wisely and diplomatically with the peculiarities of the dignified Sioux.

While the Army Officers of that day were well disciplined, well educated and were refined gentlemen, the average enlisted man of a half a century ago was not, to say the least, from the Indians' standpoint, men of high moral standing. It was the enlisted men that the Indians associated with mostly, as the officers, then as now, had their own small circle of associates and did not mingle much with the masses.

It can well be imagined just what the conduct of these common soldiers were in their far western outposts many miles from the sobering influence of church, home and women. The Indians say that gambling, drinking and lewd women were the common topics of conversation. How shocked the exhalted Sioux must have been to hear these palefaces flippantly use the name of the Great Spirit in jest, or carry on a licentious conversation in public.

The Sioux has shown much aptitude in self-government and before that duty was taken away from them and assumed by the United States, the general conduct of the tribe was admirable. If the duty of enforcing the law among themselves was again entrusted to them to the exclusion of white interference, it is believed that many desirable reforms would be forthcoming.

After only a few years of supervision, our Government allowed the Filipinos much leeway in maintaining law and order, but we have had very close supervision of the Sioux for many generations, but still we guard our authority very zealously and keep it in the hands of white people who too often are greater violators than the Indians they seek to reform.

While it is not true, as many white people living in an Indian county believe, that the Indians hate all white people, it is only natural since the Government has delegated but little power to the Sioux toward self-government, that the Indians will not extend that whole-hearted co-operation to the white enforcement officer that they would extend to those of their own race. The Indian would, if given the responsibility of law enforcement so far as it pertains to themselves, be on the alert to prevent as well as to detect crime and would be interested in creating a spirit \of obedience to the law. The young people would become imbued with the idea that it was a racial duty to obey their officials and soon their influence would be felt on the side of the law.

It can readily be imagined just what the inward reaction of the Indian is when he knows to a certainty that the white enforcement officer or even the executive officer has consumed much more intoxicating liquor on the Reservation than he has, yet the Indian is arrested and brought before the Federal Judge at Deadwood for the illegal possession of liquor and is given a fine and perhaps a jail sentence while the white officials with a "whiskey breath" leave the court room (a hallowed place the Whites tell the Indians), heads up with an air of self-satisfaction, knowing their record will show another "conviction."

What would you and I do if conditions were reversed? No doubt we would conclude that since we had suffered unjustly at the hands of the law we would give no special assistance to the peace officers, even if we had information that would help them. Until the Indians are given equal rights under the

* The author has been rather intimately associated with both races and is not willing to admit the Filipinos are superior to the Sioux.

law, we do not have the right to expect very much cooperation from them.

Congressman Usher L. Burdick, of North Dakota, in one of his books on frontier life says: "The purpose of this story is to portray some of the many wonderful traits of the Sioux women of the West. No other race of people have a deeper love for family ties and in the expression of this attribute the Sioux women are supreme."

The Sioux have, for generations, been practicing reforms that the white people have only recently adopted. The evil effects of corporal punishment in the home and in the school were recognized by our progressive educators only a few years ago, but the Sioux have known of the fallacy of such practices before Columbus discovered America. In discussing this with a group of old Indians recently, one said: "We love our children and whip our horses, it seems to us as though the paleface loves his horses and whips his children." The Indian parents at least approach the question from the right angle as they try to exact obedience and respect from the child by teaching him that a certain respect and reverence is due the parent from the child on account of the love and sacrifice that has been made for it.

Family ties are very strong among the Sioux and they are slow to see any wrong in the conduct of a close relative and no sacrifice is too great to make for a child. Indian mothers have been known to sell their best bed or even the cook stove in order to raise money to send to a child attending school away from home.

The white race only in recent years learned that the women were intelligent enough to be trusted with the ballot, but some Indians allowed their women to take part in their councils and to speak and vote more than 200 years ago. In explanation of this an Indian said that they had long ago learned that "some women are wiser than some men." They reason that since it is the woman that produces the chief, it follows that she must be about as wise as a chief.

Indians do not have to be reminded to feed the hungry, clothe the poor or give shelter to those that need it, for they do it instinctively, and do it sincerely and with pleasure. They visit the sick and the afflicted and are very sympathetic for those who suffer misfortune or disaster.

The white people and even the United States Government only during the past generation awoke to the fact that it was necessary to conserve our wild life, but the Indians have, as far back as we can trace their history, killed only that which they needed for food. The white hunter killed for the sordid pleasure derived from destroying life and even today it is only by drastic laws that the annihilating of much of our wild life is prevented.

The worth and character of a race may be judged by the actions of its soldiers in line of battle and here the Sioux have no superiors and but few equals. In defense of his own lost cause he faced death courageously and again in the World War he stood by the side of his white brother unflinching and calm. Chauncey Eagle Horn, a Rosebud Sioux, while on the battlefield of France, had his leg severed from his body by shrapnel, and as he saw his life blood gush away, he said in the Indian language to a Sioux companion, Herbert Omaha Boy, also wounded, "Tell my people that I was not afraid to die for my country."

The morale of the Sioux was at low ebb when the Hon. Cato Sells was appointed Commissioner of Indian affairs. He was a very energetic administrator and being a western man and knowing that the Indians are natural herdsmen, decided that the live stock industry presented great opportunities for them. Soon white faced cattle began coming into the Sioux Reservations by the hundreds and the Indians were happy. Individual Indians procured small foundation herds and tribal cattle were purchased for several of the reservations. Then droughts came and policies changed and the herds rapidly decreased.

The Sioux were much encouraged by a more liberal policy of government, begun in the Burke administration and enlarged upon by the Rhoads and Scattergood regime. When Mr. Collier, the present Commissioner, came into office his reputation as a friend and a crusader for the Indians caused them to expect still greater liberality and reforms. He had well defined plans as to what the Indians needed and soon began to vigorously put them into practice. Through his efforts, the Wheeler and Howard Bill was soon put on the Statute books. Mr. Collier personally took it to the Indians and patiently and painstakingly presented it to the various tribes for their approval or rejection. Most of them accepted it in whole or in part and were happy in the thought that soon they would be given more self-government. However some of the Sioux are becoming somewhat discouraged, due to the fact that a few of the higher field officers have failed to keep step with Mr. Collier's well-known ideas of self-government. Such retarding influences will be gradually eliminated when officials are found who have a high regard for and love of the Indian people and are willing to conscientiously follow the leader, Mr. Collier, in his efforts to procure more freedom for this virile race, who too long have been under the heel of oppression. On the Rosebud Reservation, where the Indians are now enjoying the more abundant life, they are making commendable progress and are happy. This is convincing proof that what the Sioux need to a greater degree is self-government. When this is accorded them they will again show their former vigor and activity. The Rosebud Superintendent, Claud A. Whitlock, is a sympathetic and kind administrator, and is a friend of the Indians, whether they be school children or adults.

There is today an unfortunate and harmful tendency at work. Newspapers, fiction writers and the movies often depict the Indian as a treacherous and sneaky race, devoid of the higher principles that go to make up an honorable people. These unfortunate gibes help to keep the public, already lacking correct information concerning the true worth of our Indian civilization, believing that the Indians are lacking the finer qualities possessed by other races. It is not thought that there is an evil plan to purposely harm the Indians but it is implied by suggestion, that the portrayal of the undesirable traits and exaggerated vices are what the public believes the Indians possess. Finally they are unkind and unjust abuses of an under-privileged people. Their true friends should make a combined effort not only to discourage but erase this false debasing and defaming of a noble race—The Sioux Indian.

****

CHIEF BIG FOOT

CHIEF BIG FOOT

Big Foot, though not a famous chief as was Spotted Tail, Red Cloud and Crazy Horse, yet he with Chief Hump exerted much influence in their day among the Indians of the Great Sioux Nation. He was a wise chief, mild mannered and always very considerate of the personal rights of his band. He was for peace, and on several occasions acted as peacemaker when rival bands were about to go on the warpath with each other. The chief had a nature not unlike that of Henry Clay, who when the dark clouds of war threatened to descend upon the people he loved, he would, with seemingly inspired wisdom, devise a compromise that would stay the dogs of war till the judgment of cooler heads would prevail.

From the account that the Indians give of him, he took the duties of chief very seriously, and was of the old type of chiefs, who lived prior to the ones that were before the public at the end of the nineteenth century; for example, Sitting Bull, American Horse and Short Bull.

He was comparatively free from revenge and was devoid of that war-like spirit that was so highly developed in many of the Sioux war chiefs. He believed sincerely that a lasting peace was possible between the Whites and the Sioux and was willing if that could be accomplished to suffer any amount of taunts or jeers from the soldiers whom he regarded as mere youths, but respected the officers who were much older men. At that time the duties of the chiefs were well defined and definite. He must see that food was in the camp and that the tents and blankets were in repair and ready for use at any time. If, through some misfortune, an Indian family were out

14

of food, the chief must see that they were supplied, even if he had to give it to them from his own tent. The widows and orphans were looked after first, and if one of his warriors lost a horse in battle or in the chase, he must see that another horse was supplied for him, even if the chief himself had to procure it from an enemy tribe. The sick were never neglected. Through his *Dog Soldiers, good order was maintained and no rowdyism was allowed. He made rules for the hunters and designated where the hunting parties should go and when they should start. If a war party was being organized he called in his sub-chiefs and head men and counciled with them before any decision was made.

Big Foot did not reach his high position by inheritance alone. In those days a chief had to prove his worth as he was growing up to manhood before he could become a leader, even though his father was chief. Leadership then was gained through personal bravery, daring deeds in battle or swiftness in the chase and by oratory and wisdom shown in their council meetings.

It is said that Chief Big Foot had less trouble between members of his bands than did chiefs of other bands because of his just ruling and unselfish motives. He himself walked upright and often prayed to the Great Spirit for help and the proper guidance of his little band.

There were only a few places of honor within the power of the tribes to bestow upon their young men so only the brightest or the most outstanding member had a chance of becoming a chief, medicine man, noted hunter, etc. The young Indians were not different from our own young white men, and many of them were very ambitious to procure these places of honor. Bravery was one of the requirements that counted for much, and from the time a boy was five years old his father and grandfather began to teach him to be ambitious for these places of distinction, and if he showed

* Dog Soldiers were tribal police who took orders from the chief and must obey him without regard to personal consequence.

that he was of a cowardly nature it was soon known among the tribe and his chance of becoming a chief was lost, and even the little Indian girls would not play with him, which also lowered his social standing.

Big Foot, as a boy, went through all these tests, and as a result was made a chief through the various ceremonies from time to time as his acts justified the honor. In addition to being a chief he was a noted hunter as well, and when the tribal supply of meat was getting low, his services were often sought by other Sioux bands. He was a skilful rider and always had a string of good riding ponies, and when his supply ran low, as it often did, from the fact that he very frequently gave horses to members of his band, he would soon recuperate his losses by making a raid on the Crow Indians or other enemy tribes. To take that which belongs to your enemy, if at war with them, is an honor in the Indian code of morals, and while the white people do the same thing, they use the word capture in place of the word steal, which the Indians use.

An Indian chief had to be an Indian leader in a moral sense as well as a leader in things that pertained to the physical side of life. A chief could not hold the respect and esteem of his band if his own conduct was not what it should be, and there was often considerable jealousy among the warriors who aspired to be chief, so it was necessary that those in command keep their reputation unblemished.

Even as a young man Big Foot was not a spectacular chief in war as was Crazy Horse and Spotted Tail, but preferred to settle disputes, when possible, in the council hall rather than on the battle field. He advocated this method in settling disputes with white people but in this he was not very successful, as the war chiefs overshadowed him in rank and many of the young warriors were often very eager to go to war to get an opportunity to prove their bravery.

16

On this famous march from Cheyenne Agency to Wounded Knee Creek, he was the head chief, and his followers were obedient and showed him great respect.

Chief One Horn was Big Foot's father, and from him inherited some of his leadership. One Horn ranked high in his generation and was chief of the Minikohoju band of Sioux Indians. In common with the custom of his tribe at that time he believed in and practiced polygamy and at one time had seven living wives with whom he lived, the Indians say, peacefully and happily. It is safe to say that he was a diplomat as well as a warrior.

Shortly after the Custer Battle, on the Little Big Horn, Chief Big Foot and two of his fellow tribesmen went to Washington on business for the tribe. On this trip, Reaches The Sky, the tallest Indian among the Sioux, accompanied Big Foot. The Indians have forgotten who the other man was, but remember Reaches The Sky because of his great height, which was over seven feet. While in Washington, Big Foot had a picture taken of himself and this is the only one in existence.

Big Foot had the distinction of being among the first Indians to cultivate a patch of corn on the banks of the Missouri River, in accordance with Government instructions.

All of Big Foot's children are dead but he has grandchildren, great-grandchildren, and great-great-grandchildren living. John Little Finger, James Pipe on Head, Jackson He Crow, George Blue Legs and Thomas Blue Legs are his grandsons, and all are men of good repute.

At the time of the Custer Battle, Big Foot and a small party were hunting in the North. Big Foot personally talked to General Custer on a previous occasion and advised him not to attempt the trip he was contemplating.

17

Several years prior to the Ghost Dance trouble Chief Big Foot and a number of other leading chiefs were in Washington on business for the Great Sioux Nation. Even at that early date the far-seeing eye of the Chief could see that there was a need for a Mission school and recommended that one be established at or near the forks of the Cheyenne River. He agreed to sponsor it and to influence his band to send their children there if the Indian Office would have it established, which they tentatively agreed to do, but for lack of a definite educational policy, the matter was pigeonholed and forgotten. Thus again Chief Big Foot was disappointed by the white man. If this little Mission school could have been established and become a community center as it certainly would with so able a leader as Big Foot at the head, perhaps the unfortunate Wounded Knee Massacre would not have darkened the pages of South Dakota's history today. Too often mature plans and policies of the Indians who have pondered over them for years, have been tossed aside by an inexperienced and immature executive in the Washington Office, placed in power by the caprice of politics.

At times Big Foot was torn between two emotions as he had faith in, and loved the old Indian ways of life yet his good judgment taught him that the new civilization that was brought to the Indians by the white people, and especially the missionaries, contained many truths that his tribe had not yet learned, then too the progressive element of his own people must be considered. When Big Foot heard that most famous Indian Speech made by Spotted Tail, he was greatly impressed, and when in the Black Hills, he and his little band meditated for days over the new line of thought given him by one of his own people. The speech of Spotted Tail is as follows:

"Alas! There is a time appointed to all things. Think for a moment how many multitudes of the animal tribes we,

18

ourselves have destroyed, look upon the snow that appears today — tomorrow it is water! Listen to the dirge of the dry leaves, that were green and vigorous but a few moons before! We are a part of that life and it seems that our time has come.

Yet note the decay of one nation invigorates another. This strange White Man — consider him, his gifts are manifold. His tireless brain, his busy hands do wonders for his race. Yet he is so great and so flourishing: There must be some virtue and truth in his philosophy. I wish to say to you, my friends: be not moved alone by heated arguments and revenge. These are for the young, we are young no longer. Let us give council as old men."

19

THE BLACK HILLS

The Indians have had numerous causes to feel aggrieved at the treatment accorded them by the white people who have been the recipients of many favors from the Indians. Hospitality is one of the many virtues of the Sioux people and contrary to the general belief of the public, they are willing to forgive even a serious wrong and bury the hatchet as they are by nature a friendly people. However, when they are wounded deeply this forgiving trait in the Indian, as in the white man, ceases to function.

The white people had successfully negotiated with the Indians for much of their hunting grounds and in every case the Government drove a good bargain and procured the land at a ridiculously low price. The Sioux who had good ideas as to the value of their land knew that they were dealing with the Government, and were lead to believe that they would receive other emoluments that would off-set the low price they were receiving and besides they wanted to show that they were friendly to the Government and that they were cooperative.

The facts are, the conservative Indians — the thinking Indians — at no time desired to dispose of any of their lands, much less the Black Hills. It was only by continual pressure on the part of the glib-tongued officials sent from Washington that the Indians ever agreed to dispose of any of their lands. They realized that already their hunting ground had been diminished far beyond the point of wisdom but they allowed Unktomi (Spider) to make them believe that land was plentiful, and that government rations would be issued.

20

The Whites had long cast envious eyes toward the Black Hills (Paha Sapa) and that had for many generations been the dream land of the Sioux. When Custer and his soldiers discovered gold there, it confirmed the oft repeated saying of the old Squatters, "There's gold in them thar hills." This discovery was made at a point where the town of Custer is now located and when the news was made public, the white people doubled their efforts to get the government to negotiate for them. The Indians were convinced that with this added incentive, the white people had the avowed intention of procuring this valuable property with the assistance of the soldiers and by other questionable methods used in coming into possession of other lands that formerly belonged to them. Previous to the discovery of gold, the Indians led by Chief Red Cloud had an agreement with the Government that it would keep all white people out of their choice country — the Black Hills — but when the announcement was made that gold had been discovered, a hord of determined gold seeking white men dashed into the hills in violation of military orders and over the protest of the Sioux people who were at that time the undisputed owners. The soldiers drove the whites out again but each time they returned and continued to trespass till the Indians decided that the Government was not trying to protect their hunting grounds and as it was their choice place to go for relaxation as well as to hunt, they felt that now the Army had deliberately failed to protect their interest and were sorrowfully disappointed.

When the prairie country failed to furnish game for them they could obtain it in the Black Hills, if not a buffalo then an elk, a deer, a mountain goat, or small game which was plentiful. The prickly porcupine could always be obtained even by a boy or a woman and it made an excellent meal for a good sized family. Wild fruits were abundant and furnished change of diet, while fish were always plentiful in the many streams. Warm winter clothing for the family was made from the skins and furs furnished by the bear, the lynx cat, the cougar, the beaver and otter. In emergencies numerous caves were available for shelter and protection. The eagle in its majestic flight over the highest peaks, uttering a scream of defiance was an inspiration to the serious minded chiefs and to capture it for their war bonnet feathers was a challenge to their prowess. Beautiful flowers grew in abundance and were enjoyed by the Indian maidens when their thoughts turned to romance. Here too, their Indian medicine men found many varieties of medicinal plants and roots which had curative qualities and were much prized by the Sioux.

While all these temporal needs were appreciated, there was still a higher motive that made the Sioux cling to the Black Hills despite all the efforts of the intruders to wrestle them from the Indians. Here under the towering spruce and pine trees, amid the sound of babbling brooks, the young mothers had given birth to their first born and the camping place was made sacred by that event. The chiefs had gathered here and the musical sound produced by the wind blowing through the trees inspired them in their meditation. The Great Spirit seemed to be with them in this favorite land where sweet sparkling pure water was plentiful and dry wood, for the campfire, was easily obtained. Here Big Foot and other chiefs had, in their younger days, rambled over the hills in quest of game or in the pursuit of an enemy and in their days of rest and recreation sat on its high hills under the protecting shadow of the towering trees and sent forth harmonious notes from their love flutes. Big Foot, felt as did the other chiefs, that it would be an evil act to barter away the Black Hills as they were surely a special gift to the Sioux Tribe from their Great Spirit. To this day the Sioux stoutly maintain that the white people living there now are trespassing. At the present time they have a suit pending in the Court of Claims at Washington, D.C., for compensation and have retained a firm of lawyers of high standing to prosecute the case which beyond a shadow of doubt is a just claim.

When the Indians were camped in the enchanting Hills, handed down to the Sioux from ancient times, romance ran fancy free, ere the pale face came to disrupt the child-like faith in these children of nature. Here the love-flute had sounded its melodious notes and had met the sympathetic ear of a Sioux maiden, who from her father's teepee was silently thrilled by her lover's serenade. The Hills were a favorite camping place for the grandmothers who, just as the sun was sinking from sight over the western hills and the moon was creeping over the eastern slopes, would gather the Indian girls in their early teens and would relate to them actual romances that had happened to her or her friends in her younger days. Perchance she would tell them about the beautiful daughter of a great chief and how she had been wooed and won and how deeds of valor had been performed by chiefs of other tribes who had heard of the great beauty of the Sioux maidens and came here to court her but had to battle with the young Sioux Indian braves of her tribe before they could get an opportunity to make love to the Sioux princess. The grandfathers, too, were influenced by the ecstasy of camp life in the Hills and would invite the boys to their wigwams, light their pipes, and as the smoke ascended into graceful curves over their heads, were inspired to tell them about Indian history and tradition that had been handed down for untold generations. The gallantry and heroism of the Sioux warriors were told to the eagerly listening boys. On other occasions they would teach practical lessons on how to make bows and arrows, how to make a lariat from skins, how to stalk wild game when hunting, or to imitate the call of birds and animals, how to find their way back to camp after the chase was over, and how to catch eagles which was the hardest of all wild creatures to procure. Then as the night grew late and the aroma of the kinnikinic, in the pipe, became exhausted, the grandfather, pipe in hand, would relate the supernatural things that are always so interesting to youth and not unlike ghost stories of the white people. He told them why the aspen leaves quiver and why the wind moans as it goes through the pine trees and what makes the mysterious sounds in the Hills, and why the wood of the cedar is red.

Little wonder then that the Sioux were often on the warpath to protect and retain their magical Black Hills and to drive off all intruders who valued them only for the gold that was in them. The white people knew little about the Sioux religion and thought of it only as a savage custom. How badly mistaken were these gold seeking commoners, for the Indian was very religious and his reverence for the Great Spirit was to him a hallowed duty. This reverence was extended to his mother • — the earth, and his father — the sky. It was sacrilegious to the Sioux to see these gold-grabbing palefaces placing gold above everything else in life. They were not only driving the game out of the hills but they were muddling the beautiful streams that heretofore were undisturbed, and they were, by digging over the hills, making places of beauty, unsightly caverns.

Finally the Government decided that the gold seekers were too numerous to drive away and made efforts to obtain the Hills from the Indians by a new treaty but to no avail. Other lands they had given against their better judgment but the Black Hills, never.

Later through fraud and deceit accompanied by a questionable treaty, procured by sharp tactics on the part of the Government it was decided that they now had possession of the Hills and from this time on the Indians were not, by the white people, considered the owners, and Alas! too often, "Might makes right." Big Foot and his chiefs knew that by rights the Black Hills were yet the property of the Sioux people, and that by their standard of right they should yet go there and hunt and dance their ancient dances and even the Ghost Dance if it suited their fancy. Why not, they reasoned they had never disposed of them and certainly had never received pay for them? Surely the mysterious paleface is a puzzling problem for the Native Americans.

MISSIONARIES

The history of Wounded Knee, from the Indians' viewpoint, would not be complete without considering the influence that the missionaries had in the affair, and the relationship existing then and now between them and the Indians in this and other phases of Indian life.

The missionaries, whether Protestants or Catholics, were selected for their special fitness for a life work which necessarily involved considerable sacrifice. The spiritual aspect of the work raised it above that of commonplace things and elevated it in the eyes of the Indians to a much higher vocation than merely earning a livelihood. Naturally the religious organizations making the selections emphasized the sacredness of the calling, and above everything else a Christian character was the prime essential. The missionaries being thus thoroughly imbued with the Biblical injunction, "Go ye therefore and teach all nations," were well qualified to go among the Sioux who were in that stage of development that needed just such workers among them.

It is regrettable indeed that the Government was so short sighted as not to realize how much it needed a higher type of employees, and it is still more regrettable that a closer relationship was not established between the Missionaries and the Government workers. This mistake is being perpetuated even to this day as the missionaries get only scant consideration from the Government employees, and while they are treated with courtesy and respect they are not, generally speaking, considered as co-workers and essential which in reality they are.

25

The Sioux people are very adept at reading character and together with their keen power of observation they soon decide, and generally very accurately, at least to their own satisfactions, whether or not the newly appointed employee is a true friend of the Indians. While there are many noble exceptions, too often the Government employee has been of a mediocre type. Higher educational standards are now required, but not enough importance is attached to the moral qualifications and occasionally an immoral and decidedly undesirable individual slips in to our services. Formerly many of the employees were brought from the South or East, depending on what political party was in power, but the advent of Civil Service has largely overcome this evil and gradual improvement is being made in the personnel.

Let it be said however that it would be difficult to over praise that minority of early employees who with meager funds and an inadequate force carried on the work so nobly in the face of almost insurmountable obstacles. Long hours were required and one employee did the work, now performed by two or three.

It was but natural that the Sioux would compare the Government employees with the missionaries, and in most instances the decision was favorable to the latter, however, the Indians have much natural politeness, hence such decisions were not discussed except in their native tongue and among themselves. The missionaries, in the olden days, soon became proficient in the Sioux language and this was much appreciated by the Indians, especially the older members of the tribe. The Government workers, through lack of interest, usually failed to master even the simplest words of the Indian language and an interpreter was always necessary which was often the cause of much misunderstanding and dissatisfaction. To a lesser degree the same evil exists today.

The missionaries visited in the Indian homes, and manifested an interest in the family. When there is sickness in camp, the missionaries are always there and these visits are

26

much appreciated by the Indians. They have prayers at the bedside of the afflicted and thus a close relationship is established. They feast with them at the marriage ceremony and rejoice with the parents when a child is born, and sorrow with them at the grave of their loved ones. This endeared them to the Indians, and gradually built up a confidence which caused the Indians to feel that in the Church workers they had real friends which in reality is true, and they make confidential reports to them that they would not ordinarily make to a Government worker.

The missionaries knew that the Indians were not planning an uprising against the whites, and Father Craft was with the Army at the Wounded Knee Camp, the night before the Massacre and assured the Army officers that the Indians were not on the warpath.

The Sioux is naturally of a deep religious nature and the Great Spirit in that day influenced a great many of his actions. The missionary brought them doctrines, different, of course, from their own, but quite similar in many ways. It required, therefore, no great stretch of the imagination for the Sioux people to adopt the white man's form of worship. The various good traits of the missionaries naturally caused the Indians to have a kindly feeling for them, and they often went to them for advice on worldly matters or for consultation of a strictly private nature. Many times, the missionaries conferred with the Indians and often disuaded them from some acts of violence or revenge, but the world in general knew nothing about it.

If the Government could have had more missionaires and christian school teachers, and fewer soldiers, the Indians would have been a thousand times better off today and Uncle Sam would not have the blood of many good Indians on his hands. If the Army officials had known what the missionaries knew about Indian life and Indian nature, or if they would have forgotten their pride and consulted the missionaries, the Wounded Knee Massacre would not have occurred. If the

27

Army officials and the high civilian officials at Washington, could have known as the missionaries knew, that the Sioux could have been conquered far more easily by love, kindness and sympathy than by bullets and broken treaties, doubtless a different policy would have been adopted. In place of arousing within the Sioux the spirit of fear, hate and revenge as the short-sighted policy of the Government had often done, a much better approach would have been the one adopted by the missionaries as a friend and helper. This developed the natural good that was in them and led to a higher realm of spiritual existence which will, it is believed, be everlasting.

The sacrifices made by the Missionaries, in the Northland, is worthy of more consideration and praise than they get from the white people in general. Sub-zero temperatures, bad roads, dim trails add to their discomfort constantly, to say nothing of the isolation, the lack of close proximity to medical and surgical facilities and being deprived of companionship of their friends and relatives.

A quarter of a century ago, the writer saw the Rev. Father Digman of the Saint Francis Mission drive into the Government Boarding School at daylight with his bay team so frosted that they appeared to be white horses. The occasion of this all night sixty mile drive in zero temperature was to answer an urgent sick call from an old Indian who had requested his visit.

The late venerable A.B. Clark of the Episcopal Church of the Rosebud Mission has often been seen with his driving team many miles off the beaten path on an errand of mercy. On one occasion, Rev. Clark did not return on time and as a blizzard was raging, the boarding school whistle was sounded at intervals, hoping that it would give him a clue as to his direction. Fortunately a trusty driving team of Indian ponies guided him on his journey to his home safely.

In recent years Father Zimmerman, though not an old man, has shown a devotion to the Pine Ridge Indians that indicates he has the old-time missionary spirit. He makes long trips to the isolated Indian camps and takes his lunch, for he will not return till late at night, but a hungry Indian generally gets the lunch and the Good Father goes hungry till he returns to the Mission. It is quite evident that hidden beneath the quiet exterior, there is the old missionary spirit of Father Digman under whom Father Zimmerman had his first missionary lessons, at the Saint Francis Mission on the Rosebud Reservation. For six years Father Zimmerman had charge of the St. Francis Indian School, the largest of its kind in the United States, and during that time the Institution made much progress.

About 24 years ago Rev. Rudolph Hertz came among the Sioux as a missionary, to fill the vacancy caused by the retirement of the good Rev. Thomas Riggs. Rev. Hertz was a young man, full of energy and adoration for the work, and immediately began to study the Sioux language, and now he often preaches a sermon to his congregation in their own language. A number of the Wounded Knee survivors are members of one of his churches.

Rev. John B. Clark, familiarly known as Rev. John, is a born missionary, having grown up on the Rosebud Reservation, where his father was for many years in mission work. Early in life he showed an interest in his father's work and upon finishing his course in an Eastern seminary, immediately returned to the reservation and his Bishop assigned him to the work formerly carried on by his father. In 1915 the writer heard him preach his ordination sermon to an Episcopal convocation. He has been among the Sioux people all these years. In his early work he was assisted by Rev. Lambert, a well-known and much beloved Indian missionary of the Rosebud Reservation.

Father Neville Joyner came from the Southland many years ago to join the missionary field of the Episcopal church on the Pine Ridge Reservation. Though now past the age of retirement he prefers to continue his life work among the

Indians. His optimistic nature, his scholarly attainments, his lovable character and gentile manners have endeared him to the citizens and his congregation.

Father McNamara, better known as Father Mack, looks after the spiritual welfare of the Catholic Indians in the vicinity of Pine Ridge. Father Mack's jovial nature and ever ready smile, together with his ability to tell an interesting story, has made him a favorite of the neighborhood. He occasionally has services at the site of the Wounded Knee Massacre, and has heard the story of the Massacre from Father Craft.

The Rev. and Mrs. A.F. Johnson labored long and hard on the Pine Ridge Reservation for a period of about thirty years, under the auspices of the Presbyterian Missionary Board of New York. Rev. Johnson made a special study of the Sioux language and became very proficient and speaks it fluently. Several members of his church were the Wounded Knee survivors. His native helper, Rev. Joe Eagle Hawk, is an Indian of much influence and one of the best orators on the Reservation.

Father Buechel, now located at St. Francis Mission School, worked with the Catholic Indian Wounded Knee survivors when he was in active missionary work on the Pine Ridge Reservation. He has made a very thorough study of the Sioux language and has recently completed a Sioux dictionary that is the most complete work of this kind in existence. He also is the author of a book of Bible stories in Sioux.

Rev. Vine DeLoria was born and reared under a missionary roof, and being himself a Sioux, is doing admirable work. Soon after graduating from college he returned to the Reservation. He has charge of both the Indian and White work at Martin, South Dakota. He is doing most excellent work among his young people. He is a good interpreter and has the happy faculty of being able to think as an Indian or go into reverse and think as a white man. He is a member of the Masonic Order at Martin and is well respected.

Rev. Dallas Shaw, a mixed blood of the Rosebud Reservation, has been in the mission work for many years. He is stationed at Allen, South Dakota and has an Indian congregation. He can preach in either the Sioux or the English language but his people prefer to hear their native tongue so most of his sermons are in Sioux. He has been a faithful Christian worker for his people and is nearing the age of retirement. His wife is a great-granddaughter of Chief Big Foot. She had other relatives in the Wounded Knee Massacre and several were killed.

Rev. Amos Ross, a highly respected Sioux missionary, spent a long life of labor among his people, and was an active worker of his church during the Ghost Dance excitement. He is now retired and lives at Martin, S.D.

Father Cunningham spent fifteen years in missionary work on Rosebud and Pine Ridge Reservations. During these very active years he was instrumental in establishing a High School for Indians at Porcupine, South Dakota. From the first, the school flourished and was much appreciated and became a community center for the Indians.

A few years ago Father Cunningham was sent to another field of work by his Superiors much to the disappointment of the Indians who cry for his return.

One of the oldest of the old-timers is Father Sialm, who has been doing active missionary work on the Pine Ridge Reservation for many years. He is very zealous and full of faith in the work he is doing. Father Sialm is a Swiss, but now his favorite language is the Sioux, and he uses it in preaching and talking to the Indians. When he first arrived at the Mission an Indian gave him the name of Black Cat Fish and to the Indians he is Ha wa Sapa.

Two young mixed blood brothers have been doing missionary work among their own people for the past twenty years and deserve special mention for their zeal for the work and the upright lives they have lived. They were educated at the Santee Mission School in Nebraska and are able to preach in either the Sioux language or the English language. Rev. Thomas Roulliard is in charge of the mission work at Okreek, South Dakota, and Rev. Levi Roulliard has charge of the mission work at Dupree, South Dakota.

Dr. Edward Ashley came from England to represent the Episcopal Church in mission work in the early seventies. At first he was located at Crow Creek, and then assumed charge of the missionary work of the Cheyenne River Reservation. He was there when the Messiah or Ghost Dance trouble occurred. Dr. Ashley was uncompromising in his zeal for his church and the Sioux, and was the star witness for the Indians in their suit against the Government for payment of the Black Hills.

Rev. Thomas Riggs deserves special credit for the manner in which he laid the foundation for missionary work for the Congregational Church on the Cheyenne River Reservation. He emphasized Character Building and Brotherly Love. After many years of faithful work he retired and is reverenced by the old-time Indians with whom he had labored.

Rev. David Clark was, like his brother John, reared in a, missionary home, and works among the Indians living east of the river, but his voice has often been heard and appreciated by the West River Sioux. In addition to his regular missionary duties, he has had charge of a Mission School at Crow Creek, South Dakota. He has also been given some of the duties formerly performed by the late Dr. Edward Ashley.

Near the site where Big Foot and his band broke camp to begin their stealthy march to Pine Ridge, lives Father Vogel, a sincere old Swiss priest, who for fifty years has lived a secluded and sacrificed life for the Catholic Indians of the

Cherry Creek district. Here he is many miles from a railroad, medical facilities and white companionship, but he, like the Indian, goes about his daily tasks in that desolate and isolated district and unconcerned about what the bustling world outside their sphere of activity is doing. Father Vogel knows all of the survivors of the massacre that live within his district and has heard the story, told to him in the Sioux language.

Three churches, the Catholic, the Episcopal, and the Congregational Church have for many years maintained mission schools on the various Sioux Reservations, and the great amount of good that has resulted from these institutions, in addition to the spiritual enlightenment, can never be fully realized. Here the upright character of the mission workers were living examples of an unselfish life. Here too, the Sioux learned culture, good manners, table etiquette, and a great many other lessons which they needed and so richly deserved.

To the churches, the Sioux owe a great debt of gratitude, for without the Church schools as trail blazers, it is difficult to conjecture just what form of educational institutions might have been forced upon the Indians. The missionaries have always championed the cause of the Indians, and more than once they have appealed to influential officials in Washington when it appeared to them that the Sioux were not getting the consideration they deserved. Strange, too, it is that only when the Indians were clearly in the right would they come to the churches or missionaries for redress. They knew, of course, that they could only expect help when the principles of right were on their side.

When the Ghost Dance religion (See Messiah) was brought to the Sioux country, quite a few of the Indians were inclined to accept the new cult and some did, but when the Government forbid the Sioux to take part in the dancing, the Indians did not go to the missionaries as they knew that it was of a questionable venture.

33

Big Foot accepted the Ghost Dance religion and permitted his band to dance at will, but did not allow any disorder nor any agitation against the Agency officials nor any disrespect toward the missionaries.

The missionaries had informed themselves concerning the new so called religion that was sorely troubling the Sioux and many other tribes as well. They knew that it was but a passing fancy and it was the wild and impossible claim that was agitating the Indians and that the truth only was needed to clear the Indians' mind of the fallacy of the new religion. The settlers and the Government employees, not knowing the Sioux language nor the psychology of the Indians, mistook their strange actions as an indication that an uprising was being planned. Some of the settlers left and went to places they thought to be more safe, and the teachers of the day schools and other Government employees, stationed in outlying districts, were brought into the Agency where they could have protection of the police and soldiers.

The Government failed to make the regular issue of clothing and reduced the beef ration to about half, and this caused much suffering among the Indians and many were shivering and half starved and came to the vicinity of the Agency, but did not know whether or not they were in danger from the soldiers. It can well be imagined the condition of affairs in these Indians' camps. They were cold, hungry and forbidden to dance as had been their custom. It would not be surprising if at times they did assume a threatening attitude that caused the Agency officials and the soldiers much concern. For a time a vigilant watch was maintained both day and night. It is worthy of note that a large number of these discontented Indians made their camp adjacent to the Holy Rosary Mission School, located five miles from the Pine Ridge Agency. The Sisters and the Priests had charge of the school, which at that time contained a hundred Indian children. The school was operated just as usual and not one of the workers left their post, but came and went in performing the daily tasks uninterrupted by the Indians.

The Government Boarding School at Pine Ridge had been deserted by the students to join their parents in the camps and after this, one of the school houses was burned.

It would have been an easy matter for the so-called hostile Indians that were swarming around the Mission to have wreaked their revenge and robbed the Mission commissary, which was well-known to be filled with provisions and there were no policemen or soldiers to guard it, but although the Indians were half starving, not one attempt at violence was made, but on the other hand the Indians sent word to Father Jutz in charge that no one there would be harmed and they were not.

THE MESSIAH OR GHOST DANCE

The white people who are not friends of the Indians, and there are many, would have us believe that the so-called uprising that culminated in the Wounded Knee Massacre, was the result of the Messiah or Ghost Dance Craze. A careful study of the question reveals that, as usual, the accusation against the Indians is wrong and that the real cause of the imaginary threatened uprising was the failure of the Government to fulfill its promises made to the Indians and failure of the Government to carry out its treaty obligations.

In order that the reader may know the history of the Messiah, or Ghost Dance, a brief explanation is given.

The early missionaries found the Sioux had a native religion that centered around the Great Spirit. This form of worship was generally accepted by all of the Sioux and they were very devoted to it. They prayed to the Great Spirit, much as we pray, but being conscientious and consistent, they went a step further and prayed for the Great Spirit to bring misfortune to their enemies. One old Indian, from the Rosebud Reservation, asked the Great Spirit to scatter his enemy's pony herd and bring sickness to his children. The white people doubtless wish misfortune to befall the enemy, but do not express the desire in their prayers.

The missionaries (see Missionary) came among the Sioux and taught them the Christian religion, and there is something in the Indian nature that caused him to readily accept this form of worship. Many of them became active in promulgating the teachings brought by the Black Robes (Catholics), the White Robes (Episcopalians), and the Short

36

Coats (Presbyterians); but at the same time retaining some faith in their own native religion, but they were not hypocritical about it as from their viewpoint, there were not many essential differences. Their great trouble, over religion, was to come in the form of the Messiah or Ghost Dance religion.

Near Pyramid Lake, Nevada, a Paiute Indian, named Wovoka, originated a new religious movement that was later termed "The Messiah" or "Ghost Dance" religion. He was a full blood Indian, who had a very limited education and spoke English brokenly. He told the Indians that on January 1, 1889, he was taken up to heaven and was instructed in this new religion, which was especially devised for Indians. Wovoka told the people that while in heaven, he was told to go back to earth and preach goodness, peace and industry to the Indians. They were to be rewarded, if they followed his instructions and would be reunited with their relatives and friends, who had died. This new world was to be a very pleasant place to live in, as there would be no more death nor sickness nor old age. While in heaven Wovoka claimed to have received instructions regarding the new dance with the admonition to take it back to the Indian people. The dance was one of the important phases of the new faith.

This new religion gained great momentum among the Indians in Nevada, and the Sioux soon heard of it. Such rumors usually became exaggerated as it is passed by word of mouth from one Indian to another, so when the news reached the Dakotas, it had grown to depict Wovoka as an Indian Messiah or a Savior. He was to restore the dead to life, return the buffalo and other game to the Indian country, and the white people were to be sent away so that the Indians could live in happiness and contentment.

Of course, Wovoka preyed upon the superstition and innocence of the Indian. He crudely devised this new religion from the Christian religion in which he had had some instruction; but it served his purpose well and as it spread among the Indians, he added other features.

The Pine Ridge Sioux would not accept this new form of worship without a more thorough investigation, but had heard so many reports of the amazing Messiah, they decided to call a great council to discuss it. Chief Red Cloud called the meeting and was assisted by Young Man Afraid of His Horses, Little Wound, American Horse, and other Sioux chiefs. It was decided to send a delegation to Nevada to learn first hand about this new religion. The council chose Good Thunder, Flat Iron, Yellow Breast and Broken Arm, from Pine Ridge; Short Bull and another Indian from Rosebud, and Kicking Bear from Cheyenne River Agency. They immediately started on their journey to the West, where they found Wovoka and apparently they were duped by his cunning story.

In the spring, they returned and brought with them a letter from the new spiritual leader, which said:

"When you get home, you must make a dance to continue five days. Dance four nights and the last night keep up the dance until the morning of the fifth day when all must bathe in the river and then disperse to their homes. You must all do it in the same way, I, Wovoka, love you with all my heart and am full of gladness for the gifts which you have brought me. When you get home, I shall give you a good cloud which will make you feel good. I give you a good spirit and give you all good things. I want you to come again in three months; some from each tribe. There will be a good deal of snow this year and some rain. In the fall there will be such a rain as I have never given you before. When your friends die, you must not cry; you must not hurt anybody or do harm to any one. You must not fight. Do right always. It will give you satisfaction in life. Do not tell white people about this. Jesus is now upon earth. He appears like a cloud. The dead are all alive again. I do not know when they will be here; maybe this fall or in the spring. When the time comes, there will be no more sickness and everyone will be young again. Do not refuse to work for the whites and do not make any trouble with them, until you leave them. When the earth shakes at the coming of the new world, do not be afraid; it will not hurt you. I want you to dance every six weeks. Make a feast at the dance and have food that everyone may eat, then bathe in the water. That is all. You will receive good words from me sometime. Do not tell lies."

Mooney, in his report of the Ghost Dance Religion, in referring to the Sioux committee that visited Wovoka says:

"All the delegates agreed that there was a man near the base of the Sierras who said that he was the son of God, who had once been killed by the whites, and who bore on his body scars of the crucifixion. He had now returned to punish the whites for their wickedness, especially for their injustice toward the Indians. With the coming of the next spring (1891) he would wipe the whites from the face of the earth, and would then resurrect all the dead Indians, bring back the buffalo and other game, and restore the supremacy of the aboriginal race. He had before come to the whites, but they had rejected him. He was now the God of the Indian, and they must pray to him and call him 'father,' and prepare for his awful coming."...Wonderful things were said of the Messiah by the returned delegates. It was claimed that he could make animals talk and distant objects appear close at hand, and that he came down from heaven in a cloud. He conjured up before their eyes a vision of the spirit world, so that when they looked they beheld an ocean, and beyond it a land upon which they say 'all the nations of Indians coming home,' but as they looked the vision faded away, the Messiah saying that the time had not yet come."

Usually an Indian committee appointed by the tribal council is very conscientious about making a true and accurate report, but in this case it must be admitted that this particular committee utterly failed in their duty and permitted their imagination to be fired by the preponderous weight of public opinion in the little circle that surrounded them. Hence they made a report that was not true. It should be remembered that the committee that was sent to Nevada to investigate the new religion was selected by a Council called by their most famous and trusted chiefs and that the men so chosen to make this important investigation for the tribe were men of high standing in whom the Great Sioux Nation had faith. That this group of trusted men should deceive their people by base trickery remains one of the unexplained mysteries of these troublesome times. Perhaps it was an early outcropping of a fifth column idea with which our own nation has to grapple with today.

The strong personality of Short Bull domineered the committee and his clever mind soon conceived the idea of becoming the Messiah for the Sioux people, and claimed to have been made a special representative of the real Messiah. Without a doubt Short Bull saw an opportunity to enhance his glory among his people, so he put forth all his power to further the cause of the new religion. Short Bull promised the people the Messiah would come in person later; but in the meantime, his resourceful mind originated new ceremonies among which was the sweat house used for purification. The interest grew and while it was stronger at Pine Ridge some of the Rosebud, Standing Rock and Cheyenne River Indians danced excessively.

Short Bull now decided on a bolder stroke and while, at first, he claimed to be only the representative of the Messiah, he now declared that he was the real Messiah.

When the Indians learned that this new religion taught that the dead was to be brought back to life, that the white people were to be eliminated and that the buffalo was to be returned, naturally the more illiterate Indians became greatly excited. Their strange actions excited the officials and settlers who thought an Indian uprising was being planned. In this the white people erred as the Christian religion taught them by the missionaries emphasized peace and brotherly love besides the alleged Messiah had specifically charged them not

40

to harm the whites. As further proof that no evil was intended toward the whites, the most ardent dancers removed to the almost inaccessible Bad Lands to continue their dancing where they would not be disturbed.

Without properly checking the situation, the government unwisely, it is now believed, sent soldiers to the Sioux country. Soldiers were stationed at Pine Ridge, Rosebud, and Cheyenne Agency; also at other strategic points. The presence of soldiers added to the excitement.

The Sioux were passing through great turmoil and physical distress. The white man had wantonly killed or driven off their wild game and the Indians were in a half starved condition. Their land had been taken away from them and even their wonder land (the Black Hills) were now in possession of the whites, illegally as the Sioux believed.

The excited condition of the Indians caused them to act very differently from the normal way of living. These unusual actions were interpreted by the strangers and white settlers as an indication that an uprising was brewing and they went to the Agency or left the country in order that they might be protected.

The minds of the poor misguided Indians were never farther from the warpath than they were then. So we see two races each thoroughly misunderstanding the other and attributing motives and characteristics to each other not possessed by either. The two races that should have assisted each other and met on a common level were far apart and ignorance, mistrust and conceit were the common enemies of both. Oh! that some unforeseen power might have intervened and shown them the truth and let the spirit of peace and brotherly love cement their friendship together!

In justice to the Indians, it must be repeated that the Ghost Dance religion, as it was, had nothing to do with the Wounded Knee Massacre except that through a lamentable error, the Government sent the soldiers to menace a people who were passing through a difficult stage of development and needed only a kind, gentle and sympathetic hand to guide them. That might have been the Government officials, or it might have been the hands of the missionaries or school teachers, and certainly it should have been the combination of the three working harmoniously together. During this very highly nervous condition of the Sioux, we find Chief Big Foot and his band camped many miles from the Agency officials, from the soldiers and from the white settlers. Their wish and natural inclination was to obey the government regulations and to be on friendly terms with the white people. On the other hand the Indian committee that was sent to Nevada to visit Wovoka, gave them strong assurance that truly the Indian Messiah was coming to relieve them from their unhappy position and that they were specifically advised to continue the dance in order that they might receive all the benefits from the new religion.

Since dancing had always been closely connected with their native religion, prior to the advent of the Ghost Dance Craze, and since Wovoka had supplied a very liberal amount of dancing in his so-called Messiah religion, it is not strange that it appealed strongly to the Sioux who had been misled by the Indian Committee who were sent to Nevada to study the new Indian religion.

More pity than blame should be extended to the bewildered Indians, whom all must agree, were woefully mistreated by the invaders as that was what the Indians believed the white people were, and in light of later developments, the word enemy would have been more appropriate. Especially is this true in regard to the various business dealings between the two races, whether it was in making treaties for their land or buying Indian products or in selling them intoxicating liquor (Miniwakan) or other commodities that the white people had to offer for sale.

THE JOURNEY

In 1890 when the Government sent soldiers to the Sioux country for the purpose of quelling an imaginary uprising among the Indians, it was the general feeling of the Indians, especially of Big Foot and his band, that it was in direct violation of the spirit of the treaty of 1868. From their viewpoint, it was the Indians who had cause to complain and not the Government.

At that time, Big Foot and his band of about 400 Indians were camped in a wild desolate wilderness on the Cheyenne River, several miles above the mouth of Cherry Creek. Though they had held many councils they were yet determined as to what they should do. They were practically without rations as the Government had failed to make the regular fall issue of food and clothing as required by their treaty obligations. They were miserably armed with old shotguns and rifles, suitable only for hunting small game; so going on the war path was out of the question, and besides Big Foot had seen, during a long life, so many young warriors lost in battle with the soldiers that he sincerely hoped that never again would he be called upon to send or lead his young braves to war.

In the midst of their bewilderment, a runner from the North rushed into camp, informing them that their great leader and medicine man, Sitting Bull, had just been killed by the Standing Rock police and the soldiers. Soon another small group of Indians arrived from Standing Rock Reservation and confirmed the report and gave more of the

43

details of the murder for that is what the Indians believed it to be then and they think the same today.

Big Foot immediately called a council and for several days they deliberated over the sad plight of the Sioux. They had done no wrong, had violated no law or regulation except that they danced, which was now objected to by the Agency officials. Their forefathers had danced for generations, but as these dances had a religious significance, surely the strange white people would not seriously object to this. However, they did object, and now the soldiers had invaded their reservations to put a stop to their dancing.

The army officials, hearing that Big Foot and his band were dancing, decided to stop them and moved a detachment of soldiers from Camp Bennett on the Missouri River, to the vicinity of Big Foot's camp. The Indians became greatly frightened as the death of Sitting Bull was fresh in their minds, so when approached by the Army officers they readily agreed to go back with the soldiers the next day. In the meantime, another troop of soldiers was seen in the vicinity and this caused greater fear among the Indians that they would be destroyed during the night.

Several days previous to this they had been considering going to Pine Ridge, where the noted Chief Red Cloud had invited them to take part in an important council, and as many of his band had relatives and friends there, a council was called to decide what to do. Two plans were discussed — one to go to the soldiers' camp and become prisoners of war, and be subjected to the whims and caprices of the Army officers and perchance be sent to a far away place as some of their chiefs had before or murdered as the great war chief, Crazy Horse, had been after he surrendered. The other plan was to make a dash at once for Pine Ridge and join their relatives and friends and be under the protection of Chief Red Cloud. Time was short, they must make the decision at once, and when the vote was taken it was unanimous that they should start to Pine Ridge that night. Big Foot was now sorely troubled, as he had promised the Army officers that he would go to their camp the next morning, and for an honorable chief to break his word to another chief, though he was a white man, was not in accordance with Indian honor. However, all of his sub-chiefs had voted to go to Pine Ridge and even a head chief would hardly dare to overrule an unanimous decision.

The spirit of freedom that caused the Pilgrims to leave the shores of the Old World to cast their lot on the strange and dangerous shores of the New World was the same spirit that impelled Big Foot and his followers to desert the prison-like reservation. Untrained and inexperienced officials at Washington had made strict and impractical rules that the Indian must obey. Here freedom of action and freedom of worship were denied the Indians, and as they had enjoyed these blessings for untold generations, it is little wonder that they decided to risk everything, even life itself. They had their own civilization, and their own customs, that were near and dear to them. The vast hunting grounds belonged to the tribe and it was their home, but now a strange people from a foreign land had invaded their country and were trying to enforce obedience to their commands. Unrestricted as they had been all their lives, such a plan was doomed to failure, and it deserved to fail.

Big Foot believed that the last step had been taken to rob the Indians of their natural heritage so without further parley, word was given to break camp and start for Pine Ridge. Being a wise chief he knew that the only chance they had to get to their destination was to get beyond the reach of the soldiers that night. He knew that with his poor equipment he had no chance of success in battle with the soldiers. In his older days he had developed a horror to open warfare with the soldiers, and now preferred the old Indian custom of getting out of a difficult situation by stealthy movements and take advantage of the darkness of night to remove his warriors from the enemy, so he planned to march to Pine Ridge.

The brightest side of the picture in taking his band to Pine Ridge was the fact that of all of the Sioux chieftans, Red Cloud had been the most successful in dealing with the Government. Through his influence the objectionable army forts in their great western hunting grounds had been removed and also many of his other plans had been approved.

The distance to Pine Ridge was great, more than 150 miles, yet Chief Big Foot did not hesitate, for as a young man he had chased the buffalo and other wild game over the intervening country and had an accurate knowledge of the streams, buttes, cut banks and Bad Lands over which they would travel. He had no compass, no maps, no roads, but only dim trails and the stars to guide him. Though the ravages of old age had sapped much of his strength, he believed that it was the wish of the Great Spirit that he lead his band to a bloodless victory to the promised land, Pine Ridge. Without further consideration, the secret word was given that the band would break camp immediately and follow Big Foot to Pine Ridge, and although all of the Indians knew of the great danger of being overtaken and captured by the soldiers, they knew about the long march, of the cold, of their shortage of food supplies, of the possibilities of a blizzard at that time of the year, and of the many other disagreeable phases of the trip. But strange not a word of objection was raised and not one Indian deserted him; so in the quiet of the winter night and unseen and unheard by the two nearby military camps, Big Foot and his band were on their way.

They silently trudged along, knowing that the military authorities would send soldiers to apprehend them if it became known that they were leaving the reservation, but the desire for justice and freedom burned in their breasts so strong that they were not daunted by the pangs of hunger or the biting blasts of the icy winds. Everyone, even the small children knew that their safety depended upon swift but silent marching till they were out of danger of being seen or heard by the soldiers. It was only natural that the Indians

46

would have very strong feelings against the Army, for it was responsible for their present suffering and danger. They had fears, that they would be captured, be murdered as had other bands of Indians in the past years. They were indignant because they knew that they had wronged no one and that they had been true to their treaty, but that the Government had not, yet it was the Indians and not the Government people who were suffering.

Big Foot now had unfortunately contracted pneumonia, but kept at the head of the band as it was he who must guide them aright. So great was his desire and determination to reach his destination in safety that he gave no thought of his own danger and believed in the justice of his actions so strongly that he felt that he had the guidance of the Great Spirit in the difficult task of rescuing his people from the clutches of the United States Army.

A few hours before daylight, they came to a protected spot and at Big Foot's orders made camp. No lights, no fire, no noise and no food, save a few scraps hurriedly gathered when they started, but soon they were sleeping. The guards were watchful and some of the most faithful were sent back a few miles to see if the soldiers were following them and were instructed to immediately give the alarm, but fortunately no dangers were encountered that night which had been remarkably quiet. Only now and then a smothered cry from a hungry baby was heard as the alert mother calmed it by putting it to her almost milkless breast.

As the stars began to fade, the sick chief sent his Dog Soldiers to awaken the camp with the instructions that they must again be on the march. The ponies had been picketed out in order that they might graze as the Indians well knew that their ability to get to their destination quickly depended, very largely, on the strength and endurance of their ponies, so they had been watered and were now ready for the new forced march. All day they marched, not stopping at noon, and only occasionally for the ponies to rest. Big Foot still weaker, but at the head of the band, guided them accurately over the hills and hollows, not daring to cause them to travel an extra mile, as he knew of their suffering from hunger, cold and anxiety.

The sun was fast sinking over the Western hills, when Big Foot with the help of his faithful wife stood up in the wagon and scanned the country to get his bearings and at once recognized a good camping place where on a former occasion, with a party of hunters, he had camped. There was wood and water and by camping on the south side of the little butte it would be a protection from the north wind. Here they made camp and as fires were now permitted and the restraint of quietness removed so the Indians and also their leader felt that they would have a good night's rest. The ponies were again properly watered and driven a short distance to a place where the grass was good and in a valley protected from the cold wind. Big Foot's contented moment was soon to be disturbed as several women with their babies on their backs carried in Indian fashion made their way to the chief's tent and timidly but pathetically informed him that they were famished from lack of food, exposure and travel, and that their breasts contained no milk, so their babies were actually starving. The tender hearted and sympathetic chief bid them come into his tent where he gave them the last morsel of food that he had. The situation was now deplorable, as the entire camp was out of food, but not wishing to add any more cares to the sick Chief had not informed him of their starving condition. Again his Dog Soldiers were instructed to make a detail of the best known hunters in camp and were told to travel East, West and South in quest of any kind of game that could be found, and in a remarkably short time the hunting party was on its way. They were supplied with what weapons and ammunition they could muster.

Among the hunters were four young men who were more adventurous than the others, and realizing that the men could not in the limited time allowed them, find sufficient wild

48

game for so many hungry people, decided to get their riding ponies and travel in a northerly direction, where they had seen herds of cattle grazing on a distant hill not very long before they made camp. So after going over the first hill that hid their movements from their camp, they struck out due north. Since the wind was from the north they could be reasonably sure that the cattle would drift south, so they soon deployed with the understanding that the hunter that sighted the cattle was to give the signal by imitating the yap of the coyote. In a short time one of the Indians came upon the cattle bedded down in a coulee. Retreating to the top of the hill, he gave the signal, and soon the four men were together again. They decided that since they had traveled north that the pursuing soldiers might be camped within hearing of a gun shot and it was decided that the lariat and the hunting knife must be the only weapons used.

One of the four Indians was detailed to hold the saddle ponies in a little clump of scrub timber near the unsuspecting cattle while the other three, one with a lariat and the other two with hunting knives, silently crawled over the hill toward the sleeping herd and stalked them, as they had often stalked the buffalo, well knowing that if the cattle stampeded there would be no beef for the starving band that night. Keeping on the windward side and hidden by the tall prairie grass till they reached the proper distance from the cattle the critical moment had arrived for the hunters. The most skilful roper was given the important task of manipulating the lariat. Could he, from the difficult crouching position that he must maintain, twirl the rope with dexterity sufficiently to place it over the horns of the large fat cow that had been selected as the victim? His steady nerve did not fail him and his aim was accurate, so the surprised and struggling critter was within their power while the remainder of the herd went thundering down the valley. The sound of the coyote yap from one of the Indians hurriedly brought the other Indian and the saddle ponies to the scene of the struggle. With skill, born of experience, the remainder of the task was accomplished in a remarkably short time and soon the men were on their way to camp each having a quarter of good beef.

The other hunters came struggling in about the same time with what they were able to kill, but it would have been totally inadequate to stay the hunger of so many ravenous appetites, so the beef fed the multitude while the meat from the jack rabbits, cotton tails, badgers, owls and hawks was cooked but saved for the nursing mothers and the children.

Preparing the meal was the work for the Indian women, and soon the meat was ready to distribute to the various families and groups. Here was the important work for the Dog Soldiers who had to divide it in proportion to the number in the family. Here again is a remarkable trait of the Sioux, as they divide the food for the camp in a way that all are satisfied. As soon as the meal had been devoured they quickly went to their tents and slept. Big Foot sent out guards in the rear to be on the lookout for soldiers but again good fortune favored them and no enemy was in sight. The night was not so quiet as the starving and yelping dogs fought over the bones and left overs, while the grey wolves, attracted by the smell of the meat, howled from the nearby hills. Big Foot awoke just before the last stars melted away from the approaching sunrise. Upon stepping from his tent he turned to the East, the West, the North and the South, and gave thanks to the Great Spirit for the safety of his camp and for the food procured the night before. He then caused the camp to be awakened and to get ready for moving immediately. The ponies had been brought in, but no breakfast was served the Indians for the reason that all had been eaten the night before except the portion which had been taken to Big Foot's tent, and as that was a liberal supply he sent for those who were nursing babies and they received a fairly bountiful breakfast in comparison to what they had been getting.

Big Foot was restless to be on his way, as one of his chiefs who had the reputation of foretelling weather conditions predicted that a blizzard would come within three days, as he had heard the owl hoot three times at sundown. Big Foot and his chiefs knew that if a severe blizzard came before they reached Pine Ridge, it would cause many deaths and much suffering among their people, so again we see Big Foot leading his band out of camp and at a little faster pace than on the preceding morning.

The day's march was rather well defined, as it was known that on the banks of Medicine Creek, good camping places were easily found and it was their hope to get there by night fall, in fact they must get there. Though hungry, they believed that the coming night would be the last time that they would have to camp on the prairie, so their spirits were improved and they urged their mounts and teams on and on, and occasionally a song here and there could be heard as they encouraged each other in their misery. Before darkness overtook them they reached the coveted place and camped for the night on Medicine Creek. They had a comfortable camp, protected by hills and timber and felt that they were out of danger from being overtaken by the soldiers, so all was well except for the fact that there wasn't any food in camp. Big Foot realized that his men were too near exhausted to expect them to go on another forced hunt, so he informed one of his chiefs to select a few of the yearling colts that yet had some flesh on their ribs and to slaughter them for food. This was done but as the Sioux's love for their horses is very great, it was only the gnawing hunger and their weakness that caused them to eat the horse flesh.

Morning came and after a brief devotion to the Great Spirit the little band was again on the march, hoping to get to Pine Ridge by night, where they knew they would be welcomed by Chief Red Cloud and by their relatives and that food would be furnished. The forced march was continued with Big Foot growing weaker, but still at the head of the procession. On and on they traveled over the dim trail that would apparently never end. The noon hour arrived but still they must move on regardless of their weakness and hunger.

51

About the time the sun was midway between the zenith and horizon, an ominous looking shadow appeared in the South. What could it be? Surely not the soldiers, for they would be coming from the North, but still the shadow comes. Hark! it is the soldiers, no mistake now as the keen eyes of the Indians soon distinguished the well-known blue uniform, the guns, the soldiers on horseback and the mule team. Big Foot could hardly talk now on account of weakness, but by almost superhuman effort he, with the help of his chiefs, halted his caravan and all were instructed to wave a white flag as a token that he came in peace.

Past events crowded into the sick Chief's memory. He thought of the fate of Crazy Horse, Sitting Bull and of the dishonorable deeds that his people believed the whites had committed against the Indians. In these harrowing moments, the old Chief remained firm in his determination to avoid a battle and while some of his followers advised resistance, Big Foot instructed his band to keep the white flags flying so that the soldiers could see them at all times. His only thoughts were now for his people and their safety and he was sad indeed.

> "His bow is broken, spirit crushed
>   To the white man's rule he must bend
> The future holds no hope for him
>   For he sees nothing but the END."
>
> — Myrtle Anderson.

THE END OF THE JOURNEY

Dark grey clouds floated over the prairie hills in the
vicinity of Porcupine Butte on that fatal afternoon of
December 28, 1890. In the far distance to the north could be
seen a melancholy, pathetic caravan of some 400 Indians
trudging their weary way over the trackless prairie. Jaded and
overburdened ponies added to the general gloom of the
picture. For almost four days this band of hunted hungry
Sioux had been traveling in the hope of escaping their enemy
and to join their friends and relatives at Pine Ridge, to where
they had been invited by Chief Red Cloud.

Why is this strange incident being enacted, Indians in their
regular way of living, before the trickery of the paleface had
disrupted and disturbed their natural mode of life would not
have considered subjecting their wives, children and old
people to the rigors of winter out on the open prairie as we
viewed them when the soldiers interrupted their journey to
Pine Ridge. The Sioux warriors faced dangers unafraid of
enemies or death, but never would they deliberately place
their non-combatants in the perilous situations that now
confront them. It was only in the hope that Chief Big Foot
could lead them to a place of safety from the soldiers that
they ventured on this hazardous pilgrimage - they trusted and
lost. In this, their darkest hour, not a word of criticism was
directed against their crushed leader, and in fact they even
yet hoped that in some way their Chief would rise to the
occasion and lead them out of their present agony. Under
normal conditions they would have selected a permanent
winter camp in a sheltered nook, where wood and water

53

would be plentiful. Here the Indian women would have had dried meat and a bountiful supply of wild dried fruits, pemmican, Indian turnips, etc. They would not have failed to provide their winter camp with medicinal plants in the way of roots, shrubs, leaves and other Indian remedies that experience had taught them of their value in sickness. To their food stores would have been added from time to time, fresh venison or other meat from local game as the hunters returned from the chase. Good tents supplied with buffalo robes and the skins of other animals would have been made ready for the stinging north winds that the Sioux knew were sure to come each winter. As an additional protection, the tents in which there were babies and small children a thick mat of woven willow brush would have been placed on three sides of the tent. Dry wood piled high at each tent would have assured comfortable quarters for all, even though it was zero weather. Each night the love flute would have sounded from a nearby picturesque butte, the merry laughter of many playing children would resound over the hills and hollows. On special nights, the tribal dances would have brought renewed life to the adults or a council of the chiefs would have brought interest to the camp. Hunting parties returning from a successful day's hunt would enliven many occassions, scouting parties would go out from time to time from these winter camps, and return with a drove of horses taken from the Crow Indians, the enemies of the Sioux. The stories of adventures of the young brave warrior in the making was always listened to very attentively and would inspire the young Indians with hope that they too might soon be allowed to go out on scouting parties and perform similar or greater deeds of bravery. Religious dances each week would have put the camp in a more serious mood and devotion to the Great Spirit would have been a part of the camp activity.

Let us return to Big Foot and his present dilemma, where we left him and his band, halted with the white flag of truce flying, as they viewed the steady and determined approach of the soldiers. The blue clad enemy came charging upon them as if immediate total destruction was uppermost in their minds, but regardless of the war-like manner, not one of the Indians made any hostile like movements, but held the white flags high in the air as the old noble Chief had instructed them.

The Indians well knew from the actions of the soldiers when they first met them that revenge was uppermost in their minds. The snappy commands of the officers were quickly obeyed, and they deployed as if to form a line of battle that the Indian warriors had seen on many other occasions. Even the machine guns were put in place ready to fire. In face of the facts that the Indians were displaying many white flags, the Army officer's West Point training was so strong that he could not do otherwise than seek the leader and demand their surrender, and with a detachment of soldiers he approached the place in the Indian line that looked like it might contain the leader. The Indians instinctively pointed to Big Foot, who had now by special effort managed to sit up in his wagon.

The pompous Major Whitside denied the sick Chief the honor of a parley, but with his forces deployed ready for battle, demanded of Chief Big Foot an unconditional and immediate surrender. Since it was not a war party and resistance was out of the question, every request that the Major made was agreed to, as Big Foot realized it was not the time or place for argument. Through the Army interpreter, the Indians were given explicit instructions to march into camp, at Wounded Knee Creek, where the remainder of the Army was stationed.

Chief Big Foot waved a feeble arm with a forward motion and all the Indians moved on in the same direction that they had been traveling, and soon the word reached those in the rear that they were to go in with the soldiers and camp on the Wounded Knee Creek, and that the next morning they would be permitted to go on into the Pine Ridge Agency. There was silent rejoicing among the few Indians who had faith in the soldiers, but the Chief was not so optimistic, as he felt much misgivings, though he kept up his courage, so as to give confidence to the rest of the band. Slowly the march continued but now with less spirit than before, as they were under the orders of the soldiers. We see weary eyed mothers, gaunt and sad warriors, half famished children, hollowed eyed aged Indians with bowed heads and subdued expressions following the white captors to camp.

What was in store for them? Would they be murdered as was Sitting Bull and the Great Warrior Chief Crazy Horse, would they be returned to Cheyenne River Agency from where they had left and be treated as prisoners with all liberties taken away from them? These and many other thoughts were surging through their minds as they silently but sullenly obeyed the commands haughtily given them by the soldiers in charge of the march.

The most puzzling thing was the fact that the soldiers came from the South as they were expecting to be apprehended by soldiers from the North from whom they had escaped when they started on the march to Pine Ridge. Surely the ways of white people were mystifying and beyond the understanding of these primitive Americans. Why should these soldiers from the South interfere with their rights to travel in their own country? These poor bewildered people were within the bounds of the Sioux reservation, which was theirs by right of original ownership and so regarded by all the Indian tribes, theirs by right of a treaty with the intruding white people and yet they were put under arrest by the powerful Army and must suffer the taunts and insults of the soldiers. But alas! they were in the hands of Custer's old command, the Seventh Cavalry of the United States Army.

Would this painful and silent march never end? The suffering from cold, hunger and fatigue caused from the long march, was now having its telling effect on all the band, but to the aged, the suckling mothers and small children, the fatigue was more than they could long endure. Even the leg weary ponies and dogs moved foreward with difficulty and hesitated, and it appeared that the mental depression of the Indians had in some way affected these dumb animals.

The rapidly descending sun and the cold blast from the North warned them that night was fast approaching, but when they reached the top of a hill the sight of the soldiers' camp on the Wounded Knee Creek gave them hope and every ounce of reserve strength was called into use and they moved faster. Soon they reached the designated camping place and very soon the Indians had their tents erected and their ponies watered and driven off to a nearby grazing site. The heart of the Great Chief was all but broken as his mad dash for liberty that he had always known, had, as he now believed, failed and it was with humiliation that he accepted a comfortable tent the commanding officer so graciously offered him. It was not for himself that he was thinking but for his band that had so fully trusted him to lead them to Chief Red Cloud for protection. He too thought of the importance of the Council of Sioux chiefs that were waiting his arrival to begin their discussion on the disputed question with the Government. He knew of the importance of the Council and had very definite ideas of how it might result in bettering his people's condition if he could only get his band to Pine Ridge and then Council with Red Cloud and other Sioux chiefs and offer his conciliatory plan. The confidence that he had in his own Great Spirit and the faith he had learned to have for the White People's religion had buoyed him up to this point, but now a strange feeling was coming over him, was it his physical condition that caused him to falter and to distrust the white people, more than ever before? Was the sickness and suffering robbing him of his faculties? He fought desperately to clear his mind of the fog that threatened to engulf him as he realized that he was facing the greatest crisis of this long life, he knew not what to do, so he prayed.

JENNIE RUNNING EAGLE
(nee Afraid of Enemy)
died 3/23/1936

THE LAST NIGHT

On account of the stirring events that had occurred on the various Sioux Reservations, by the sudden appearance of many soldiers together with the excitement incident to the Ghost Dance Religion and the killing of Sitting Bull, of the Standing Rock Reservation, caused great excitement through the Sioux Reservations. When the details of the manner in which Sitting Bull was murdered were learned by the Indians, the excitement grew in intensity. He was the greatest of all medicine men and in addition was a prophet in whom they had great faith and they now looked upon his death as another wicked and cruel deed of the great strong United States Government.

The Army was very active on the Cheyenne River Reservation and were forcing the Indians to stay within the bounds of certain designated territory. Big Foot's band had heard that many Indians had slipped away from the soldiers and were in the Bad Lands, and were participating in the forbidden Ghost Dance Religion, and that the soldiers of the Rosebud Reservation were making Indian life precarious. These strange acts of the Army and officials had been very distressing to Big Foot and his chiefs as they camped for the first time, virtually prisoners of war, yet there had been no war. Inwardly they were very much disturbed but outwardly they kept a cool demeanor.

On this eventful night, the last night, Big Foot's band was sleeping on a sight selected by the soldiers whose guests or prisoners they hardly knew which they were. A limited amount of rations had been issued to them by the commanding officer and Big Foot had been shown much courtesy and had been given the needed medical attention by the Army physician. The next morning they were to break camp, they believed to join their friends and relatives in Pine Ridge. None of the band except Big Foot and his chiefs realized the seriousness of their arrest and the remainder of the Indians were looking forward to having a happy visit at Pine Ridge the next day. Their appetites had been partly appeased and they now had hopes that in the morning they would be issued sufficient rations for breakfast. Many of the Indians and the women especially thought they had been invited by the Army officers to share the camp for the night and surely they would not let their guests go away hungry. It was but natural therefore, that the general gloom and the forebodings that had been their constant companion for days and weeks would now subside and that they would enjoy the blessings of a night of peaceful sleep. No longer did they fear the soldiers from Cheyenne River Reservation would overtake them and force them to return as prisoners. Then too the fact that they were almost at the end of a long journey, had a stimulating effect on the entire camp. Success was they hoped and dared to believe within their grasp, one more short march and they would, if floating rumors were true, be free to roam at will and live their own lives in their own way. This optimism was, of course, not shared by Big Foot and his confidential chiefs, who well knew of the danger they were yet to pass through before being allowed to continue their journey to Pine Ridge. One cloud had not been dispelled from the camp as their beloved Chief Big Foot was yet suffering intensely and they vainly wished for the service of their great medicine man, Sitting Bull, whose skill they never doubted, but was now still in death at the hands of the race which was rendering medical attention to Big Foot. They, of course, had but little faith in the white doctor and who could blame them?

Here we have two camps within a few rods of each other, two races, two civilizations, two religions, two sets of moral codes, two sets of ideals and two purposes in life. Let us take a view of the two peoples. The soldiers' tents were lined up in military order, the cavalry horses, sleek and blanketed, munched their hay and oats in contentment while the big rugged Government mules, staked out with West Point precision, bit and kicked each other in a playful mood. Supper had been served on time, cooking utensils and dishes had been disposed of in the usual military fashion. The officers' tents were pitched a short distance from and back of the enlisted men, the tent ropes were taut, and canvas showed not a wrinkle while inside the heat from the small stove radiated comfort. All wool Government blankets, piled high added to the prospect of a comfortable night by men who held the fate of the other camp in their hands. No doubt, the officers as well as the soldiers were discussing the Indian situation and perhaps enlarged upon the imaginary danger that they were in from the prostrate Chief Big Foot, and his woebegone and disheveled followers. "Remember Custer's Massacre" and "Revenge for annihilation of the Old Seventh Cavalry" and other expressions were in common use and designed to instill hatred for the Sioux in the breast of the new recruits who had but recently arrived in the Indian country.

The Indian tents, ragged, patched and dirty were pitched somewhat irregularly and with but little uniformity, and the inside showed every sign of poverty. Robes, skins and blankets badly worn had been thrown in the corner while a scant fire in the center of the tent filled it with smoke but not much heat. Some of the Indians were cooking supper, some were eating while others had finished. Tired, sick and crying children, lean and half starved dogs, haggard and weary Indian ponies made up the Sioux camp.

Taps were sounded and the soldiers' camp became quiet, and all tent lights were extinguished and the Indians out of respect for the military rule became less noisy. The braves after a visit to the chief's tent, had gathered in another tent

61

to council on vital questions, now lowered their voices but continued to talk and smoke until late into the night. The ever alert chief too sick to meet with them had given instructions as to agreeing on plans about breaking camp that would not be in violation of any of the soldiers' rules. Indian mothers had returned to their own tents to make preparation for the night, buffalo robes and blankets were placed for the various members of the family. Even the unusual conditions that existed here on this last night did not prevent the mothers from arranging the beds of the various sleepers in accordance with the Sioux custom in which the pallets or bed were assigned in the order of age and sex.

The steady tramp of the guards that surrounded the camp, the keen click of the bayonets and the sharp command of the officers could be heard in the stillness of the night when the guard was being changed. The Sioux must have marveled at all these war-like maneuvers and wondered why all this precaution was necessary when there was no thought, at least on their part, of war or a surprise attack. The Indians were taking no such actions but they decided it was just another one of the foolish whims of the white race, and except for the customary horse wranglers their camp was unguarded.

The midnight hour had arrived, the swains had returned to their tents and the lovelorn maidens drew their robes around them and ere sleep robbed them of consciousness, thought of the young chiefs who on other and more suitable occasions and surroundings had played the love flute for their special entertainment.

The grandmothers, ever alert for the safety of their children, especially for the marriageable daughters, were the last to seek rest. Long years of experience and vigilance had taught them that they could not always trust their own young men much less could the white soldier be trusted, especially when the charms of a beautiful Indian maiden were the prize. These grandmothers had also learned from the experience of many winters that even the well trained maidens from the best Indian families were not immune from the mating call.

Across the prairie, the howl of the wolf was heard and across the canyon its mate answered, and the sulking coyotes took up the cry and made the night hideous by the wicked wail of the howling pack. Indian mothers in Big Foot's camp, lying in their chilly tents, heard the howling and instinctively drew their sleeping infants nearer to them and cuddled them closely, fearing that harm might come to them, never dreaming that a far greater danger was much nearer than the wolves, and that on the morrow instead of the fangs of the wolf the little bodies of their babies would be pierced by bullets from the guns of the soldiers of the United States Army, and that the mothers would be ruthlessly killed and their unarmed warriors shot down like rabbits.

Big Foot, yet seriously sick, lay in an Army tent suffering excruciating pain at every breath, thought of his faithful followers and painfully glanced at the East to see if there was any sign of the coming day. What would the new day bring forth? Would it be liberty and the blessings of friends and relatives or would it be betrayal and death as it had been to his long faithful friend, Sitting Bull?

The Chief's wife had been awakened by his growing restlessness and knew from the chirps and calls of the birds that it was almost time for the light to appear in the East. She assured him that all was well with the camp and urged him to sleep so that he would be ready for the trip to the Agency at the head of his band, so for the first time during the night Big Foot slept. The sub-chiefs rested but little during the night as they feared for the life of Big Foot, who was growing weaker and his fever increasingly higher, then too they thought of the safety of the camp but would reassure themselves that they were under the protection of the friendly Government. Did not the treaty of 1868, which the chiefs knew by heart say in Article One, "From this day forward all war between parties of this agreement shall forever cease. The Government of the United States desired peace and they pledge their honor to maintain it." Thus consoled they too slept a little, not realizing that the treaty of 1868 could be a mere scrap of paper. The shrill notes of the bugle sounded reveille and both camps were immediately astir and the last night for Big Foot and his band, was ended.

THE MASSACRE

The braying of the Army mules and the fading darkness indicated that a new day was dawning and this gave Big Foot renewed hope that he might yet see his band safe with their friends at Pine Ridge, and that he would once more sit in the council with the mighty Sioux chiefs, with Red Cloud at the head. Here again, they would deliberate upon new and important questions that meant so much to the Indian people, and if not wisely and satisfactorily adjusted, meant unhappiness if not the doom for the great Sioux Nation.

The morning broke clear and cool, the mute hills that had witnessed so many tragedies in the animal world, gave no warning that a human tragedy, that would cause the profound sympathy of all Christian Americans, was about to be enacted. The wild things seemed to question the right of the unusual gathering but kept well back in the scattering pines of the nearby hills. The great, red, round sun appeared over the Eastern horizon and Big Foot thanked the Great Spirit for bringing them through the night safely. He had spent a restless night but by his strong willpower had kept his mental faculties clear though racked with pain and exhausted from fever and exposure. He seemed to have a premonition that some evil was about to befall his band. Throughout the night he had prayed for the deliverance of his people from the hands of the Army. He tried to have faith in the white people and their treaties, but so many broken promises and so many failures on the part of the Government caused him to have doubts and forebodings.

When the bugle sounded reveille and its clear notes echoed and re-echoed through the hills, the Indians wondered if it was an ominous warning. Soon the camps were astir and anxious to finish the routine work. The Indians were eager to be on their way to Pine Ridge and they, like their indomitable leader, were in great suspense but happy in the thought that they at least had hopes of being freed from the designing clutches of the United States Army. Surely if the soldiers had intended to do them harm they would have taken advantage of the darkness as they had done in other occasions, so they ate a scant meal and continued their preparations to break camp.

The soldiers, under strict discipline, had completed their morning details and duties with alacrity, and were now ready for the more serious work of the day. Just what was on their minds is unknown and history can never reveal it. Was it revenge for the Custer defeat on the Little Big Horn? Was the motto "Remember the Seventh Cavalry," embroiling their minds and steeling them for a grim deed? Was an awful national crime being contemplated against the Government's hungry and abused wards? The Army officers well knew that the Indians were at their mercy and that a sure victory was theirs, if they chose to make the kill. Can it be that an ambitious Army officer, like Custer, had visions of military fame by wiping out this band of Indians camped a stone's throw from his soldiers. Subsequently events plainly indicate that some dark and subtle plot was hidden beneath their strange maneuvers.

The slogan that, "the only good Indian is a dead Indian," was more often quoted then than now, and did much harm and prejudiced many whites against them, and was used as propaganda to poison the soldiers, who had just come to the Indian country, against an imaginary foe.

But hark! the commanding officer is sending out new orders. A hush, a quietness reigned for a moment. The orders were for the Sioux to approach the center and deposit all

66

their arms, at a designated place. A signal from the sick chief, caused the braves to obey the order. But alas! greater insults were to be heaped upon them. Soldiers were ordered to search the tents, wagons and bedrolls, for arms. The women were searched, all axes, crowbars, knives and awls were taken from them and deposited with the guns. Helpless indeed were these now worse than destitute Indians as they could not kill or skin small game for their food and could not put up nor repair their tents. Such unreasonable demands had never before been enforced and were resented by the Indians and especially were the Indian women amazed at the interference with their packing and taking their camp utensils, but a gesture from the Chief, commanded silence.

Big Foot and his chiefs believed that these acts may have been an effort on the part of the soldiers to provoke a quarrel but they were determined to remain true to their treaty and to the white flag of truce which they carried. If Chief Big Foot had the remotest idea of fighting the soldiers, he would have done so when they first sighted the army near Porcupine Butte. Here he could have sent his warriors to the small scattering buttes in the vicinity and made a creditable showing in the kind of warfare to which they were accustomed. Certainly such a plan would have sent Major Whitside scurrying back for reinforcements at which time the entire band could have slipped to the nearby Bad Lands where pursuit would have been difficult if not impossible. They knew of course by this time that any show of resistance meant certain death to the band as they were now wholly defenseless.

What further demands could now be made by the soldiers for an excuse to wreak their revenge? The white man's history says that one of the Indians resisted being searched and during the scuffle, his gun was discharged and that this immediately brought forth an attack from the soldiers. The Indian survivors dispute this story and it is just as reasonable and more so for the Indians to say that a soldier fired a gun as a signal for a general attack, as it appears from the Indian evidence that immediately after this alleged firing of the gun, that there was a general attack made on the Indian camp. Even the Hotchkiss guns, on the hill began firing. The synchronous firing from all sources is very strong proof that the soldiers were on the alert ready to fire on a moments notice, this included the infantry, the cavalry, and the Hotchkiss guns. It appears therefore that they anticipated trouble even if they had to start it themselves. It is difficult to conceive of how the soldiers could imagine the Indians would start a fight under their well known handicap. The army officials knew of the poor guns and lack of ammunition in the hands of the Indians as they had a chance to observe them the day before as they marched into camp. Then, too, every word and act of the Indians was one of peace and submission. Did they not immediately hoist a white flag as soon as the soldiers were sighted, and did not their chief assure the army officer that he was a man of peace, and did they not keep a white flag flying continually from the time they camped till it was shot down by the soldiers. Again if the Indians had any intentions of fighting, surely they would have removed the women and children from the danger zone — Indians never subject their families to the dangers of battle.

James Mooney, an unusually careful writer, in his report on the massacre says:

"At the first volley the Hotchkiss guns trained on the camp opened fire and sent a storm of shells and bullets among the women and children, who had gathered in front of the teepees to watch the unusual spectacle of military display. The guns poured in two-pound explosive shells at the rate of nearly fifty per minute, mowing down everything alive. The terrible affect may be judged from the fact that one woman survivor, Blue Whirlwind, with whom the author conversed, received fourteen wounds, while each of her two little boys were also wounded by her side. In a few minutes 200 Indian men, women, and children, with 60 soldiers, were lying dead and wounded on the ground, the teepees had been torn down by the shells and some of them were burning above the helpless wounded, and the surviving handful of Indians were flying in wild panic to the shelter of the ravine, pursued by hundreds of maddened soldiers and followed up by a raking fire from the Hotchkiss guns, which had been moved into position to sweep the ravine.

There can be no question that the pursuit was simply a massacre, where fleeing women, with infants in their arms, were shot down after resistance had ceased and when almost every warrior was stretched dead or dying on the ground. ———————— the wholesale slaughter of women and children was unnecessary and inexcusable."

Another writer, Herbert Welsh, who was unusually exact in his writing, says: "From the fact that so many women and children were killed, and that their bodies were found far from the scene of action, and as though they were shot down while flying, it would look as though blind rage had been at work, in striking contrast to the moderation of the Indian police at the Sitting Bull fight when they were assailed by women."

The scene that followed was so ghastly that words fail to depict the revolting sight. Mother and babes wallowing in their own blood, while another was carrying a lifeless infant and leading or dragging a bewildered child. A father in the throes of death crawling around in a dazed condition endeavoring to find and unite his family; lovers wounded and in their dying moments whispering each others name.

The dead soldiers were soon removed from the field by their comrades and the wounded soldiers were immediately given medical attention, but not so with the wronged and suffering Indians. The soldiers were too busy looking for hidden Indian women and children to kill rather than render relief to their fallen foe.

On New Year's day, January 1, 1891, three days after the massacre when the soldiers had been given sufficient time to celebrate and to gloat over their unholy victory, a detachment of soldiers was sent out to the scene of their recent crime, to bury the Indians and to bring in the wounded if perchance any had survived after the snow storm which culminated into a blizzard. Any one knowing of the severity of a South Dakota blizzard can hardly believe that the resistance of any human being would be sufficient to live three days, in a wounded condition, exposed to all the furies of the storm. Nevertheless the soldiers found a number of women and children alive though all were badly wounded or frozen or both. Most of them died after being taken to the emergency hospital at Pine Ridge.

Four babies were found under the snow, wrapped carefully in shawls by their dying mothers who, in their last moments, thought of their loved ones and cuddled the little bodies close to their own for protection and safety. At least one of the babies lived and grew to manhood and is a trusted employee at the Rapid City sanatorium, where he has a happy family consisting of a white wife and two children.

It is difficult to ascertain the exact number of Indians that were killed and wounded, but General Mills reports that the Indian agent in charge of Pine Ridge at that time thinks there were three hundred Indians killed, while General Colby says that there were 100 men and 120 women and children found dead on the field but quite a few of the dead had been removed by the Indians themselves, especially is this true of the babies and children. The number that were wounded will never be known as many of the Indians were wounded but never reported it, and did not receive any medical attention but, of course, were given all the aid and comfort possible by their own people in the camps.

BUFFALO IN WILD STATE
Photographed by L. A. Huffman, Miles City, Montana

AFTER THE MASSACRE

During the night following the massacre, a cold north wind arose and later snow began falling, and when morning came the scene at Wounded Knee had changed completely. In place of the dull drab criminal setting of the night before, mother earth was covered with a pure white glistening snow; the soldiers, too, had disappeared, perhaps anxious to get away from the scene of their wicked deed that was in strange contrast with the purity suggested by the spotless snow. The Indians believe that the Great Spirit had sent the snow to cover the physical traces of the grim crime that the soldiers of the United States Government had committed against the Sioux people.

The soldiers, after wreaking their revenge, had returned to Pine Ridge agency that evening and, of course, their dead and wounded had preceded them, where the wounded could be given additional medical attention and the dead could be given a respectable burial.

Most of Big Foot's band, who the morning before were active and in anticipation of joining their friends, were in a way happy but now they lay covered with snow, except a very few who had a spark of life left but were so badly wounded that they were unable to speak and were too chilled to move. There were no sounds of life and the death-like stillness was foreboding. Here and there on the adjoining hills could be seen an Indian mother with disheveled hair wailing or singing the death song and calling the name of a loved one whom she well knew lay somewhere beneath the blanket of snow. Only recently they were members of an organization

72

of Native Americans living as their civilization had taught them to live. They had their families, their relatives, their friends, their property and their place in society, they loved and were loved, they were ambitious to progress along the lines that their ancestors had taught them which was the only method they knew in which they had faith.

The dead were scattered over a large area of land as the soldiers had pursued the fleeing women and children and shot them down. Many of the seriously wounded had died during the night and their groans and wailing caused by pain from their lacerated bodies and frozen flesh had echoed over the hills and valleys in vain till death mercifully ended their sufferings.

The third day the blizzard had subsided sufficiently for the people to get to Wounded Knee. Friends, relatives and the curious were there. Soon the rumbling of wagons were heard in the distance and in a short time several four horse mule teams drawing army wagons loaded with soldiers appeared on the grounds. One detail went to the top of the hill to the place where the Hotchkiss guns had been placed for battle. Here they began digging a trench about fifty feet long, six feet wide and six feet deep. Another detail accompanied the mule teams went in search of the dead and when found the frozen corps were thrown into the big freight wagon like so much cord wood and when the wagon box was full, it was driven to the trench and the bodies were tossed in with no more feeling than if they were unloading sacks of grain. There were no caskets, no ceremony, no tears, no prayers; but jocular remarks were made as the Indians were thrown in the pit. Off they would go again for another load, singing and jigging as though they were not in the presence of death. It is wondered if they were still happy in the thought they were still avenging the death of Custer and his battalion.

Big Foot, the Chief, was shown no more respect than

anyone else and it is not known in what part of the trench he was buried.

After the battle of the Little Big Horn, the Indians, 'tis said, went over the battlefield, took the clothing and valuables found on the dead soldiers, but when they came to General Custer, out of respect for the leader, his body was not disturbed. In death, the Indians recognized and respected rank and leadership, but not so with the soldiers at Wounded Knee.

The white soldiers had previously taken their wounded and dead into Pine Ridge followed by the army, and it can readily be imagined how they marched into camp with that proud and haughty air as if to say: "See the conquering heroes," but in the still quiet hours of the night, their meditations must have been very different as they thought of the fleeing women and crying children that they so ruthlessly shot down in their mad desire for revenge. The words of Lady Macbeth when she reflected on the horribleness of her deed, would in her mad ravings say: "Off, off dam spots," would have been quite appropriate for these men who the Sioux say and believed murdered the Indian women and children.

The wounded continued to come in or were brought in to Pine Ridge for several days, as some of them had wandered many miles from the scene of the disaster. The Episcopal Church had been made into an emergency hospital. The members of families who were not wounded kept up a diligent search for the missing members. Sometimes they would find a child seriously wounded and in the hospital, or if only slightly wounded was being cared for by a relative. Too often, they could get no trace of the lost child, husband or wife and then were forced to the conclusion that they met death and were lost to them forever and were now in the long trench, placed there by the soldiers who had killed them. Some of the Indians saw the soldiers who so unfeelingly tossed their relations in the graves. More than two hundred were buried here, but no one knows the exact number nor who they were except those whose names appear on the monument. The Indians call this the graves of the unknown Indians.

The heartless manner in which the detail of soldiers buried the dead is, the Indians feel, another proof that revenge was the guiding factor that caused the massacre. Common decency would have demanded that there be at least some resemblance of a Christian burial even though they were a vanquished foe. With the Indian scouts available and some of them present it would have been an easy matter to make individual graves and given them numbers and names so their relatives might know where their loved ones were buried. There were missionaries on the reservation who would have been glad to conduct funeral services if they had been given an opportunity or the Army chaplain was available, and surely he would not have refused his services even though he was a member of the organization that was responsible for the deed.

The Indian relatives and survivors have placed a cement curb around the trench graves and erected a monument on which are the names of Indians, but these are only the most prominent ones and many women and children rest there unrecorded. The following apt inscription is on the monument, together with the names of the known braves that met death by the atrocious act.

This monument is erected by surviving relatives and other Oglala and Cheyenne River Sioux Indians in memory of the Chief Big Foot Massacre December 29, 1890.

Colonel Forsythe in command of United States troops.

Big Foot was a great Chief of the Sioux Indians. He often said I will stand in peace till my last day comes. He did many good and brave deeds for the white man and the Red Man. Many innocent women and children who knew no wrong died here.

The erecting of this monument is largely due to the friends and relatives of Joseph Horn Cloud, whose father was killed here.

Horn Cloud, the peacemaker, died here innocent.
Courage Bear
Crazy Bear
December 29, 1890, CANKPE OPI EL TONA WICAKTE PIGUN HE CAJEPI KIN.

The names of those who were killed at Wounded Knee:

1. Chief Standing Bear
2. Mr. High Hawk
3. Mr. Standing Bear
4. Long Bull
5. White American
6. Black Coyote
7. Ghost Horse
8. Living Bear
9. Afraid Of Bear
10. Young Afraid Of Bear
11. Yellow Robe
12. Wounded Hand
13. Red Eagle
14. Pretty Hawk
15. William Horn Cloud
16. Sherman Horn Cloud
17. Scatter Them
18. Red Fish
19. Swift Bird
20. He Crow
21. Little Water
22. Strong Fox
23. Spotted Thunder
24. Shoots The Bear
25. Picket Horse
26. Bear Cuts Body
27. Chase in Winter
28. Roots Its Hole
29. Red Horn
30. He Eagle
31. Lodge Skin
32. No Ears
33. Wolf Skin Necklace
34. Lodge Knapkin
35. Charge At Them
36. Weasel Bear
37. Bird Shaker
38. Big Skirt
39. Brown Turtle
40. Blue American
41. Pass Water in Horn
42. Scabbard Knife
43. Small Like Bear
44. Kills Seneca

GRAVE OF WOUNDED KNEE VICTIMS

COMPENSATION

The Wounded Knee Massacre was so horrible and the results so terrible that those who have learned the real inside facts and have a love for justice, now feel that it is the solemn duty of the Government to contribute something to alleviate the suffering of the survivors and make the last years of their lives more bearable.

Feeble attempts have been made from time to time, by the survivors, to persuade Congress to make an appropriation for them and thus provide funds so that they who are in the winter of life could have at least the bare necessities, but as they had very few white friends at that time that cared to assist them, no results were obtained. Even their local agency at Pine Ridge and the Indian Office in Washington did not champion their cause.

Claims that the Indians file against the Government, like most other Indian business, are not as a rule, given very serious consideration by the citizens or by Congress and there are two main reasons for this. First, the Indians have been so outrageously mistreated and have had so many claims disapproved because of race prejudice and lack of proper presentation that the people have learned to look upon these claims as not being worthy of consideration. Second, from a voting standpoint, the Indians are unimportant, owing to the few Indians, in comparison to the white voting population. Regardless of these failures the survivors, knowing the justice of their claim, are again asking for compensation.

Congressman Werner, who was a member of the seventy-third and seventy-fourth Congress, introduced a bill for the relief of Big Foot's band, but in the midst of so much relief legislation for the whites, Mr. Werner's bill, much to his disappointment, received but scant consideration from Congress.

Mr. Francis Case became a member of the seventy-fifth Congress, and being from South Dakota, took up the fight for his Indian constituents. The Committee on Indian Affairs of the House of Representatives, held a hearing on the bill, and while it did not get to the House before adjournment, some progress was made and Congressman Case hopes that further consideration will be given the bill by the present Congress.

Secretary Ickes is favorable to some form of relief legislation; the Commissioner of Indian Affairs, John Collier, always a devoted and sincere friend of the Indians, where so ever found, hopes for this bill to pass, and if this one fails he is favorable toward other relief legislation for the Wounded Knee survivors.

It is hoped that a more compassionate Congress, led by the few members who have made a study of the Indian question and know of the wrongs that have been heaped on the Indians, may give sympathetic attention to the cry for justice of the Wounded Knee survivors. Among such an honor roll of lawmakers can be included Congressman Case, South Dakota; Congressman Burdick, North Dakota; Congressman Coffee, of Western Nebraska; Congressman Mundt, of South Dakota; Senator William Bulow Sr., Senator from South Dakota; Senator Wheeler, of Montana, and Senator Gurney, Junior Senator, South Dakota.

There are other public spirited men living in or near the Sioux country that have the milk of human kindness in their hearts and hope that the Government will adopt a permanent safe and sane policy that will advance the cause of the Sioux and do justice to the Wounded Knee survivors. Among this number should be mentioned Hon. Gutzon Borglum, a sculptor of international fame; Tom Berry, stockman and twice Governor of South Dakota; Theo B. Werner, editor and twice representative in Congress; George Phillips, lawyer and United States District Attorney; Les Jensen, lawyer and ex-Governor of South Dakota; Millard Scott, editor and Rural Credit Director; John Linehan, stockman and bank president; Dr. Theo Riggs, physician and surgeon; Prof. E.P. Wilson, historian and college professor; Judge William Willamson, lawyer and Representative in Congress for twelve years; Sam Young, scholar and ex-Indian Service Superintendent. These are practical men who know real Indian life as it exists on the Reservations today, they know of the hunger, the sickness, the heartaches, the disappointments of a conquered race. To the above list could well be added an Indian, William Berger, a mixed blood Indian, who knows, as no white man can know, the inner thoughts of the Sioux people.

The amount requested is insignificant, considering the seriousness of their grievance, but the War Department apparently has a watch dog in Washington whose special mission is to prevent this modest claim from receiving favorable consideration. The only logical reason for the Army objection to this claim being allowed is the fact that it would be conclusive proof that the Seventh Cavalry, Custer's old command, did make a military blunder in murdering its prisoners after they had surrendered. It is perhaps only natural that the Army would not admit of so glaring a mistake, and is content to object and then refer the people to the report made by the Army officers at the time of the massacre. It should be remembered that this report was made by the same officers that made the error and are accused of the grave deed of firing into the band of surrendered Indians, including women and children. The report did not fail to mention the bravery of the soldiers.

It is now believed that the survivors and those who love justice will be able to present a case that would convince any unprejudiced court of the merits of their claim. Surely the testimony of the survivors, honorable Christian Indians, should be admitted as competent evidence. They welcome the most searching investigation and are willing for the white light of publicity to be turned on the Wounded Knee Massacre.

In addition to the Indian testimony, they can furnish statements from white people and some of the Army officials, and the Indian scouts who were present, and have made statements that plainly indicate the massacre was unjustifiable, and that there was a desire for revenge against the Sioux Indians.

We quote from an editorial by John Collier, Commissioner of Indian Affairs, printed in the April number of Indians At Work, in 1938:

"Visits by groups of Sioux Indians to Washington in recent weeks have brought into view many interesting situations.

"The Wounded Knee Massacre survivors have come. What a beam of light they and Representative Case, of South Dakota, speaking in their cause, shed upon a mournful phase of Indian history, now forty-six years in the past. Those who are closely interested may obtain the departmental report of the pending bill which would compensate the survivors of the massacre. Three paragraphs are quoted here.

"The Wounded Knee incident properly has been called a 'massacre.' The historical facts are here set down as a basis for judgment by the Congress.

"The unrest and distress among the Sioux bands had increased in its intensity through a number of years prior to 1890. The causes of the Sioux misery need not here be recapitulated. There had been ruthless violations of treaties and agreements, and numerous administrative abuses. It scarcely was possible for the Indians themselves to know what spots they were permitted to inhabit and what they were forbidden to inhabit, so sweeping and so casual had been the violations and unilateral abrogations of contract on

81

the part of the Government. One of the responses of the Sioux Indians, as of numerous other tribes similarly distressed, was the flight into Messianic religious revivals, the Messianic revival among the Sioux was known as the Ghost Dance Religion.

"It is important to note that these Messianic revivals had taken place from time to time for many years among the Indian tribes, and in no instance had they thrown the Indians into aggressive warfare with the whites. Neither acts of war, not massacres nor depredations, had resulted from the numerous Messianic revivals. This record was known to the Government at that time.

"Four hundred Sioux, in family groups (whole families with all their transportable possessions), assembled for the Ghost Dance ceremonies, were shot down by Government troops – mass firing into the congregation, and then an individual man-hunt (and women and baby hunt). General Miles wrote: 'The official reports make the number killed 90 warriors and approximately 200 women and children.'
"This, all this was in the olden
Time, long ago."

In these terms we are accustomed to think of Indian wrongs. But not so – the Wounded Knee Massacre was almost now."

Major McLaughlin, author of "My Friend, The Indian." and for fifty years a worker among the Sioux, said: "It is apparent that the blankets, saddles, ceremonial paraphernalia, and the surviving animals of the Indian victims were taken possession of by other parties, immediately following the slaughter of most of the owners of the property. The Army was in complete possession of the field at the time, hence the Government must be held responsible for the operations of loot which followed the massacre."

James Red Cloud, hereditary chief and a grandson of the renown Chief Red Cloud, was in Washington, D.C., at the time the Indian Committee of Indian Affairs was considering the Wounded Knee Bill, and was invited to speak before it.

The Chief said, in part, "In compliance with the orders of the United States Government and the Army, where they made these treaties with us, we laid down our arms. ...At one time we held the entire country that you own today. Although those treaties were made prior to that killing, you came in here and murdered and slaughtered our babies. You made a pledge through the treaty that anybody who committed an offense shall pay the penalty or compensate for same, and that is all we are here to ask for — compensation for the survivors of Wounded Knee."

Honorable Will Rogers, Chairman of the Committee on Indian Affairs in the House of Representatives, desired to be informed on the merits of the Wounded Knee Massacre bill that had been referred to his committee, addressed a letter to the Secretary of the Interior and received communication which is copied herewith:

Washington, D.C.,
April 12, 1939.

Hon. Will Rogers,
Chairman, Committee on Indian Affairs,
House of Representatives.
My Dear Mr. Chairman:

Further reference is made to your request for a report on H.R. 953, which would recognize a liability of the United States for certain Indians killed or wounded in the affair at Wounded Knee Creek, South Dakota, between the Sioux Bands of Big Foot and Hump and troops of the United States on December 29, 1890.

H.R. 953 is similar to H.R. 11778 introduced in the Seventy-fourth Congress, and H.R. 2535, Seventy-fifth Congress, but not enacted. These facts are described at some length in report of this Department dated April 28, 1937 (contained in House hearings on H.R 2535).

The bill, H.R. 953,would authorize an appropriation in the name of each victim, killed in the Massacre, of the sum of $1,000, and in the name of each victim wounded in the Massacre an equal amount to be paid to the survivor or to be distributed among the heirs. The date of the Wounded Knee Massacre was December 29, 1890, or 49 years ago. The Massacre can be viewed both as an injury to the individuals who were killed or wounded and as an injury to the entire Sioux Tribe. Redress, therefore, could be attempted through the method of pensioning individuals or through creating some new advantage for the tribe as a whole, as, for example, a more generous relief to the indigent and infirm or the establishment of an orthopedic hospital for all the Sioux.

In reporting on H.R. 11778, the Seventy-fourth Congress, the Acting Director of the Bureau of the Budget transmitted to this Department a copy of a lengthy communication addressed to him by the Acting Secretary of War recommending adverse action on this bill.

The Acting Director of the Bureau of the Budget had advised that the proposed legislation would not be in accord with the program of the President.

> Sincerely yours,
> (Signed) HAROLD L. ICKES,
> Secretary of the Interior.

It is not believed that the humanitarian President, who on many former occasions has shown a benevolent spirit toward an under-privileged class, would, if apprized of the burning injustice, suffered by the Wounded Knee survivors, object to this bill, but rather would he give it his blessing.

It is surprising too that even a cold calculating budget director would recommend against this bill which would in a small measure compensate at a small cost to the Government a little group of outraged Indians for a wrong suffered at the hands of the United States Army. Why should this Director of the Budget have gone to the trouble of passing on the written objection made by the Acting Secretary of War, to the Congressional Committee who were considering the bill? What chance have these helpless survivors for justice against an array of Army officials plotting to prevent favorable legislation for them? Would it not be better for the War Department to throw a mantle of charity over any mistakes that they think the survivors have made and allow the small pittance to be granted? Certainly there would be less said concerning the military blunder that was made at Wounded Knee, and the unfortunate affair would not be kept alive by the Indians who will not cease their vigilance till the wrong has been corrected.

On March 13, 1917, by General Nelson A. Miles. General Miles, addressing the Commissioner of Indian Affairs wrote in part:

"In my opinion, the least the Government can do is to make a suitable recompense to the survivors for the great injustice which was done them and the serious loss of their relatives and property.

"The action of the commanding officer, in my judgment at the time, and I so reported was most reprehensible. The disposition of the troops was such that in firing upon the warriors they fired directly toward their own lines and also into the camp of the women and children, and I have regarded the whole affair as most unjustifiable and worthy of the severest condemnation."

Since about thirty soldiers were killed and the same number were wounded, the Army has tried to give the impression that this was the work of the Indians, but the facts are the Indians say that they were disarmed and the soldiers were killed by their own men. This is a reasonable conclusion as there were soldiers among the Indians searching for weapons, and as the fire was directed at the Indians, of course, some of the soldiers would have been killed. Testimony from the Kent-Baldwin report following an investigation of the Wounded Knee Massacre is positive proof that the Indians are correct in saying that the soldiers were killed by their own bullets. It is only natural that an Army of men, with revenge in their hearts, would make such an error, but to blame it on the Indians is an old trick of the white people.

Camp of Second Battalion, Seventh Cavalry
On Branch of White Clay Creek

January 9, 1890, 11 A.M.

Present: Major J. F. Kent, Fourth Infantry, and Captain F.D. Baldwin, Fifth Infantry. Colonel J.W. Forsyth, Seventh Cavalry, was also present. Captain C.S. Ilsley, Seventh Cavalry, was called and being duly sworn testifies as follows:

"I commanded the Second Battalion of the Seventh Cavalry during the engagement on the Wounded Knee on the 29th of December, 1890.

"Q. Were your troops so placed on the morning of the battle as to be out of danger from the fire of other troops?

"A. From my remembrance of the location, E Troop of the battalion was located out of danger of fire from others. G Troop's position was the safest, I regard, of all. D and C, I think their position was such as to receive the fire from other troops.

"Q. Under all the circumstances attached to the work of the day, referred to, do you consider that the disposition of the troops was judicious?

"A. I don't think it was, I think in the disposition of the troops the troops should have been on one side and the Indians on the other.

Pine Ridge, South Dakota, January 10, 1891, 10 A.M.

Captain Allyn Capron, First Artillery, being duly sworn, testifies as follows:

"I was on duty in the field at Wounded Knee Creek, South Dakota, in command of four Hotchkiss howitzers, caliber 1.65, manned with detachments of light battery, E, First Artillery, forming part of the command of Colonel J.W. Forsyth, on the 29th of December, 1890.

"Q. Do you think the troops were judiciously located?

86

"A. I think it was unavoidable that some of our own troops should be hurt from our own fire, but I could not swear definitely that such was the case. I neglected to state that Lieutnant Hawthorne, of the Second Artillery, was attached to my command and was wounded in the engagement."

Pine Ridge, South Dakota, January 10, 1891, 1:30 P.M.

Charles B. Ewing, assistant surgeon, United States Army, was then called in, and having been duly sworn, testified as follows in answer to questions:

"I was present at the battle of the Wounded Knee with Big Foot's band of Indians on the 29th of December 1890. I have reason to believe that some of our men were killed by the fire of other of our troops. I base it from the position of the troops. The most injury was inflicted upon Captain Wallace's Troop K, and there was another troop which suffered almost as severely, I think it was Captain Varnum's Troop B. One out of every eight was wounded or killed taking the number of troops to be 50 strong each. There were about 25 killed from all the troops and a large number wounded; located as the troops were and firing as they did it was impossible not to wound or kill each other."

While the sub-committee on Indian Affairs was in session Major Ralph Case was requested by Congressman Case, of South Dakota, to speak. He said in part, "I am attorney for the Sioux tribe; however, I do not appear here in the capacity of an attorney. This particular slaughter of women and children and unarmed men was, to my mind, so outrageous, that we would not under any circumstances accept anything in the way of attorney's fees from this Survivors' Association. For that reason, we prefer that the record should show that this is one Indian claim that is not formented nor engendered by attorneys for the tribe, but comes solely from the people themselves.

87

In 1876, troops moved from Fort Abraham Lincoln,North Dakota, and from Fort Tellerman, Wyoming, into Montana. Those expeditions were intended to drive the Sioux Indians from hunting lands reserved to them under the treaty of 1868. That was a most unfortunate campaign by Generals Crook and Custer against Crazy Horse, Gall, Two Moons, and several other Sioux chieftains. It was a campaign in which a large number of Sioux lost their lives, and in which Custer, with 212 men, lost their lives. General Custer was in command of the Seventh Cavalry, and the men who lost their lives at the Battle of Little Big Horn, on July 25, 1876, were members of the Seventh Cavalry.

After that campaign, General Miles went into this territory and succeeded in excluding the Sioux, and following that Congress passed a statute taking away from the Sioux Tribe the entire Black Hills. Now, from the Black Hills area, which is the richest 100 square miles in the world, came over $400,000,000 of mineral value.

During the Major's speech the following conversation took place:

Mr. Francis H. Case. At that point, Mr. Chairman, may I call attention to the report of the Secretary of Interior, which quotes this from the narrative of General Miles:

"Not only the warriors, but the sick chief, Big Foot, and a large number of women and children who tried to escape by running and scattering over the prairie, were hunted down and killed. The official reports make the number killed 90 warriors and approximately 200 women and children."

Mr. Barton. Major, you emphasized the fact that it was a Seventh Cavalry that was in the Custer Massacre?

Mr. Ralph Case. I did.

Mr. Barton. And that the Seventh Cavalry engaged in the Wounded Knee battle was the same Seventh Cavalry. Did you mean to intimate that there was a spirit of revenge that had been passed down in that outfit?

Mr. Ralph Case. I did mean to intimate that, and I will show you, Congressman, that the commanding officer was Major Whitside. At the end of the late war I served under his son, who was then Lieutenant Colonel Warren W. Whitside, and while this is not good evidence, nevertheless I will say for the record that Colonel Whitside told me that the Seventh Cavalry went to Pine Ridge with full intent of getting even for the loss of Custer at Little Big Horn, 14 years before.

Mr. Francis H. Case. Of course, Mr. Chairman, a point I would like to keep clear is that the Seventh Cavalry under Custer at the Little Big Horn in 1876 was a military expedition invading Indian territory, while at Wounded Knee in 1890, Indians moving with their families under a flag of truce were in the process of surrendering to the military, and unarmed women and children were pursued and shot down, without a chance to defend themselves. a desire to even scores may explain but does not justify what happened."

For the unmilitary like behavior of the soldiers and the lack of proper placing of them, the commanding officer, Colonel James W. Forsyth was court-martialed and for a time was deprived of his command. The fact that he was accused by his superiors is sufficient evidence to prove that the whole affair was irregular and put the stamp of disapproval on his actions.

Is it possible that the Army of today, our own Army in which we have a justifiable pride, must for the sake of loyalty to the Seventh Cavalry, defend this unmilitary act in which its prisoners were slaughtered? Substantial Indian evidence and public opinion is now on the side of the survivors, while the Army can produce no evidence, save the reports made at the time by the officers who were reprimanded for unethical military tactics. Naturally then they would try to make a defense but in this case it is very flimsy evidence and not substantiated by some of their brother officers who were present. The statement of the great, good and wise leader,

89

General Nelson A. Miles, should in itself be sufficient to convince the world that the Wounded Knee affair was indeed a massacre and not a battle.

Regardless of what the soldiers say or what white people may write, the Indians, and especially the survivors, who know all the facts, will go to their graves pointing an accusing finger at the United States Army. One survivor, a grandson of Chief Big Foot, stood with bowed head looking on the graves and said: "Until the Government makes restitution, these dead will continue to speak."

Although Congressman Case is doing all that is humanly possible, for he is truly a friend of the Dakotas, to procure favorable action by Congress on the bill for relief to the survivors, the writer is of the opinion that approval of this bill will be withheld by the present Congress. The fact that this fall (November 5, 1940) there will be an election in which all the members of the House, one-third of the Senate and a President of the United States will be elected, is of sufficient importance to delay action on this bill. The sudden return to economy on the part of the Government and the new plan for defense will discourage Congress from taking action.

When the new Congress convenes, January 3, 1941, it is believed a new and more practical bill should be introduced, providing the survivors approve of such action. If the new bill would provide for a special pension for the remaining 42 survivors of say $60 per month it would insure them the comforts of life, which they have not had since the date of the Massacre and it could become available immediately. The question of damage for lost property and relatives could be given subsequent consideration after the actual participants and sufferers are provided for. They are poor, old and in ill health, and sorely need relief now.

It has been proven by statements of the survivors that the Sioux, at no time, had any intention of resorting to arms to the soldiers and that they took the precaution to keep the flag of truce flying at all times. The evidence further shows that the soldiers under orders from the officers, went to the tents and searched the bed rolls, tents, wagons and even the women for additional weapons, and that they took all the equipment that could in any way be used as a weapon, such as knives used for domestic purposes and awls that the Indian women used in repairing their tents, etc. It was just at this stage that the soldiers opened fire on the Indians who were now defenseless and helpless. The Indians did the only thing that any one could do, by attempting to escape without making any pretense to fight, as the odds were so much against them.

No other instance in history of the United States Army, so replete with deeds of valor and heroism, can be found where the prisoners, after surrendering and being disarmed, were fired upon and killed. It follows therefore that such an act being contrary to all the laws of civilized warfare, the responsibility for the loss of life and property should be placed on the United States Army and that suitable compensation, even at this late date, should be speedily made.

Consideration should be given to the element of revenge which the evidence shows was in the heart of the soldiers of the Seventh Cavalry, yet Chief Big Foot did not take part in the Custer Battle and his only offense was in being a Sioux Indian.

In appealing to The Congress for relief of the Wounded Knee survivors, may we remind you that they have no press reporter, employ no lawyer, seldom use the telegraph wires and do not know the meaning of the word lobbyist; so their story has been unknown to you and the general public. Think of the multitude of claims that come before you, many of them with but little merit, and compare them to the claims of the Wounded Knee survivors with the evidence they have submitted in their personal statements. Forty-two survivors come to you with outstretched arms, imploring relief at your hands — the only place this side of eternity where they may receive justice.

The following pages represent the voice of the Survivors of Wounded Knee, and while it is drastically different from the Army reports, made immediately after the Massacre, and likewise it is different from the newspaper reports printed soon after the incident, but it should be remembered that reporters sent to cover this assignment could get their information only from the officers and the soldiers. That this was decidedly a prejudiced source of information, all must admit. The soldiers knew beyond a shadow of doubt that the slaughter was unprovoked and that revenge was uppermost in their minds when they were making the kill. If they could lead the public to believe that the Army had performed a patriotic act and that great heroism had been displayed, the real truth might be concealed and to make heroes of the soldiers, and treacherous villains of the Indians, was the proper propaganda to place before the public.

The Indians tell a straight story with but few inconsistencies and is as free from exaggeration and prejudice as you could reasonably expect, considering the lapse of time and the enormity of the offense. It is true that the Indians spoke from memory, but those who have been closely and sympathetically associated with the Sioux people will testify to the fact that the old Indians are gifted with remarkable memories and have a natural desire to be truthful. Then, too, the very nature of their blood curdling experiences would make a mental impression upon the survivors that will not be eradicated till their dying day. People do not forget when they see their fathers, mothers, sisters, brothers, wives, husbands and children murdered by the United States Army. They do not forget when their bodies are riddled with bullets, they do not forget when they lay wounded for two or three days in a fireless cabin without blankets or food in a South Dakota blizzard, they do not forget when they know that their frozen dead were tossed, unfeelingly, into a trench by the soldiers who murdered them.

JAMES PIPE ON HEAD

DEWEY BEARD

STATEMENTS OF SURVIVORS

The Sioux, in their natural way of living uninfluenced by the necessity of being put to their wits end to cope with the wiley whites who had come among them, had high ideals and their morals were models that the frontiersmen would have done well to emulate.

To falsify, before their own people in a sacred meeting of this kind, opened with prayer would be an offense to the Church or their Great Spirit. Their statements were looked upon as semi-sacred as they knew their words were being recorded and would be printed for future generations to read. Sioux do not hold up their hands to God with perjury on their lips.

Dewey Beard (Indian name, Wasu Maza) is the only living man who was in both the Custer battle and the Wounded Knee Massacre. He was seventeen years old when Custer made his last stand and while Dewey was not one of the regular warriors he, with a number of other Indian boys, took part in the battle.

Though 77 years of age, Dewey is well preserved and very active. He rides horseback and wrangles his own herd of ponies. During the past tourist season he with his family moved temporarily to the new Bad Land National Park, where he sold Indian curios to the tourists. He is a full blood Indian and a man of influence among his tribes. His account of the Massacre appears below:

DEWEY BEARD
WILLIAM BERGEN, *Interpreter*

I was a member of the band that was killed here. Just a little beyond Porcupine Butte we were coming this way when we were met by the soldiers. Big Foot, who was sick and had been sick then for four days, had a hemmorhage, came up with a flag of truce tied to a stick. We were traveling in a peaceful manner, no intention of any trouble. I was told that this was an officer that came around to where Big Foot was laying, so I followed him up possibly a yard right behind him. I wanted to know what his intentions were. This officer asked Big Foot —"Are you the man that is named Big Foot and can you talk?" He asked him where he was going. I am going to my people who are camped down here. The officer then stated that he had heard that they had left Cheyenne River and the Army was on the lookout for him. "I have seen you and I am very glad to have met you. I want you to turn over your guns." Big Foot answered, "Yes, I am a man of that kind." The officer wanted to know what he meant by that, so the interpreter told him that he was a peaceful man. He says, "you have requested that I give you my guns, but I am going to a certain place and when I get there I will lay down my arms."

"Now, you meet us out here on the prairie and expect me to give you my guns out here. I am a little bit afraid that there might be something crooked about it, something that may occur that wouldn't be fair. There are a lot of children here." The officer then said they are bringing a wagon and I want you to get in that and they will take you down to where we are camped. Shortly a wagon drew up and they wrapped a blanket around him and placed him in the wagon and started to camp, so we followed. This side of the store, where you see these houses, is where we were camped and right this way is where the soldiers were camped. In the evening they unloaded some bacon, sugar and hardtack in the center and stated that someone should issue this out, so the

95

women all came into the center and I am the one that issued it out to them. We heard a mule braying over this way and also heard the soldiers making a complete circle from the south to the north direction. I forgot something too that I wanted to repeat. That evening I noticed that they were erecting cannons up here, also hauling up quite a lot of ammunition for it. I could see them doing it. Shortly after we erected our camp, guards were stationed around. They were walking their beat. I also noticed that night besides the store there was some fires built there and we knew that they were the Indian Scouts. The following morning there was a bugle call, shortly after that another bugle call, then I saw the soldiers mounting the horses and surrounding us. Even though they had surrounded us and we noticed all these peculiar actions, I never thought there was anything wrong. I thought it wouldn't be no time until we could be starting towards the Agency. It was announced that all men should come to the center for a talk and that after the talk that they were to move on to Pine Ridge Agency. So they all came to the center. Shortly after that I also followed and came to the center where they all were gathered. After I got there and looked around and the men were just sitting around unconcerned. Big Foot was brought out of his teepee and sat in front of his tent and the older men were gathered around him and sitting right near him in the center. The interpreter said that the officer said that yesterday we promised some guns and that he was going to collect them now. I don't remember how many soldiers there were, but these soldiers were climbing on top of wagons, unpacking things, taking axes and other things, and they were already laid down. Some of the Indians were further east that had guns in their arms but were not seen for some time. They were out over where the soldiers were so finally they called to them to bring their arms to the center and put them down. One of them started towards the center with his gun. This fellow that started said: "Now it was understood yesterday that we were to put down our guns after we reached the Agency, but

96

here you are calling for our guns so he took the gun and showed it to them." He started towards the guns where they were laid down and one soldier started from the east side towards him and another from the west side towards this Indian. Even so, he was still unconcerned. He was not scared about it. If they had left him alone he was going to put his gun down where he should. They grabbed him and spinned him in the east direction. He was still unconcerned even then. He hadn't his gun pointed at anyone. His intention was to put that gun down. They came on and grabbed the gun that he was going to put down. Right after they spun him around there was the report of a gun, was quite loud. I couldn't say that anybody shot but following that was a crash. The flag of truce that we had was stuck in the ground right there where we were sitting. They fired on us anyhow. Right after that crash, that is when all the people were falling over. I remained standing there for some little time and a man came up to me and I recognized him as a man known as High Hawk. He said, come on they have started this way, so let's go. So we started up this little hill; coming up this way, the soldiers started to shoot at us and as they did High Hawk was shot and fell down. I wasn't so started back and then they knocked me down. I was alone so I was trying to look out for myself. They had killed my wife and baby. I saw men lying around, shot down. I went around them the best I could, got down in the ravine, then I fell down again. I was shot and wounded at the first time I told you that I fell. I went up this ravine and could see that they were traveling in that direction. I saw women and children lying all over there. They got up to a cut bank up the ravine and there I found a great many that were in there hiding. We were going to try and go on through the ravine but it was surrounded by the soldiers, so we just had to stay in that cut bank. Right near there was a butte with a ridge on it. They placed a cannon on it pointing in our direction and fired on us right along. I saw one man that was shot with one of these cannons. That man's name was Hawk Feather Shooter.

NELSON A. MILES REMEMBERS DEWEY BEARD

This is to certify that twenty-two years ago I gave Dewey Beard a certificate of good character and am much gratified to learn that he has maintained that character ever since. He is one of the survivors of the Wounded Knee Massacre, in which he was twice seriously wounded and lost his father, mother, two brothers, sister, wife and child killed.

I recommend him to the sympathy and kindness of all.

(Signed) NELSON A. MILES,

Lieutenant General U.S. Army.

Pine Ridge Agency, S.D., October 21, 1913.

JAMES PIPE ON HEAD
President of the Survivors Association
HENRY STANDING BEAR, *Interpreter*

These people coming from the other reservation reached the foot of the Porcupine Butte. At that point they realized that the soldiers were going that direction to meet them or take them by surprise, or whatever it may be, so Big Foot, who was my grandfather, was sick and his wife was driving the wagon. Big Foot told these people to raise the white flag; that means peace. So on a stick they fixed a white flag and they carry it. The old man advised these people that if the soldiers meet them they must not be disturbed, the Indians must not start anything; that was the old man's advice at this place. An armed officer, with an Indian interpreter, told them that the soldiers were camped down on Wounded Knee and took Big Foot and his band down there. Big Foot was camped at some point on Medicine Root the night before they reached the Butte. That day they came down here and the soldiers took Big Foot off to one of the soldier's tents for care. The night I first visited my grandfather and some of the Indians visited him. The next morning the Indians were issued a little hard bread for rations and then following that there was a request or call that all the Indian men should get

98

together in some spot or some point, which they did. I was a boy, my grandmother asked me to take some tobacco over to Big Foot where he was lying, so I took it. Of course, at that time the Indians were completely surrounded by both cavalry and infantry. I delivered the tobacco to the old man, and he was lying there in the center of all these Indians who were called together. That is where I delivered this tobacco to him. At this time, all of the Indians were unarmed, all their weapons taken from them and Big Foot told me that I had better go back to grandmother and to where the women folks were. Just at this moment there was a big noise; I couldn't see just what it was but it was sounding like quite a number of gun shots together. This I knew it was guns fired on us. When these soldiers started shooting, I started to run towards the hillside over there at a distance I came across a little boy. I took the little boy by the hand and all at once someone came on the side of me and took hold of my hand. This woman was my mother. She had a baby on her back, my sister, but this girl that she was carrying on her back was shot, while we were running we saw on the ground dust flying, some of the bullets struck near us. We managed to get around through the line and escape through this direction.

ROUGH FEATHER
69 Years of Age
HENRY STANDING BEAR, *Interpreter*

I am going to just tell about the way that they surrounded us, right below here, and I am going to tell only that which I saw, and the things I heard will be the only things that I will tell about, also my activities and how I came out alive. Right down here, all the Indians were placed in a group and were surrounded by the soldiers. So I had a blanket on, don't know where I got it from, someone gave it to me, I covered my head up and stood there among them, and I understood that the soldiers wanted the guns. I was facing that way and I could see Big Foot, he was lying in a tent. Right near where Big Foot's tent was I saw a soldier. He had his gun in his hand, and in a loud voice made some remarks. So I looked over at him. It may be possible that very soldier is still living. He was the one that again said something in a very loud voice. About that time I heard some noise behind so I looked back. I saw them aim the guns at us. It sounded much like the sound of tearing canvass, that was the crash. As I heard the crash I became unconscious. Something struck me. As I was standing there I happened to look up and the smoke was awfully dense, but I could now make out a face right in front of me. As I saw him he turned and started the other way so I followed. As I started to follow him I saw him get in front of the soldiers and grabbed hold of one and they both fell down together. I was right up on them and I had to jump over them. The other soldier standing nearby struck me with his gun in the chest. I missed something that I wanted to state. That soldier that hit me with his gun from the effects of that my breast bone here is smaller and thicker. I ran down along the flat down here towards the cut bank. As I was nearing the bank it frightened me to hear some Indian calling my name. "Come," he said, "as fast as you can, it is terrible." The man that said that was Ghost Bear who is still living. I believe that man is the cause of my living today. He said again, "There are a lot of women and men laying down over here you had better go over here and lay down." So I went down there where they were laying and stayed there with them. Shortly after that they ceased firing. Then again I heard someone say, "All of you that are still alive get up and come on over, you will not be molested or shot at any more." I heard them state that, but I was still a little bit afraid so I just remained there. The second time he repeated that, well then I got up. They told us to come in a bunch to where they were so I started that way and I ran into a man. His face was all covered with blood. The man had a gun and, of course, he looked horrible. So I just stopped and stood there. Then the man came up to me and asked where he was shot. This man said that there were seven men that were shot or wounded. So I went up to a wagon that was pretty well loaded, but I took it. He told

100

me again, "These are some of your relatives laying here, they are not dead yet but you better put them on the wagon." I didn't know who they were but I started to load them on the wagon. I recognized one, an old small lady who was the wife of Big Foot. This man that I told you that had his face all bloody that was giving me these instructions I believe that man is still living and his name is Philip Wells, who is called in Indian, the Fox.

LOUISE WEASEL BEAR

You can see me, I am sick and I hurt every day. The soldiers nearly kill me. I never done them any harm or any other white man. That Massacre was very wrong to the Indians and Big Foot didn't want to fight the soldiers. He always had a white flag so that they would know he was for peace and for the treaty.

The soldiers did not fire in our camp till the guns were put down at Big Foot's teepee. Before they shot us some of them came to our tents and wagons and the women. They took our knives and axes. After this they killed us and our children. We tried to run but they shot us like we were buffalo. I know there are some good white people, but the soldiers must be mean to shoot children and women. Indian soldiers would not do that to white children.

GEORGE RUNNING HAWK
54 Years of Age
HENRY STANDING BEAR, *Interpreter*

The first thing that I heard, was a voice saying all men must come to the center to talk. These are just the very words that I heard. My father, I heard him say that the soldiers were asking for guns and he took his gun and started for them and told me to look after the horses. So I caught up the horses and tied them up. Quite a while afterwards, I also went over to where the gathering was. The first thing that I saw was the guns that were piled up. I was sitting near a man who told me that just as soon as the talk was over that we were going on to Pine Ridge Agency. Shortly my father came over and told me that I had better return to the camp and look after the horses, so I went back to camp again and saw nothing wrong with them, so I came on back again. I looked around and could see where the women were picking up and getting ready to move. I saw soldiers there throwing out stuff from the wagons and getting all things that could be used as weapons and looking for things. Yesterday we were out here to visit when it rained and there was a flash of lightning. We all got up and everybody ran for shelter — the flash or crash that we heard here was worse than that. I jumped and looked round — nothing could be distinguished, everything was smokey. I was going to start the other way and a man that I was sitting with was knocked over and shot and I had to jump over him. I became unconscious, lost my mind. First thing I became conscious like, I was down here at the creek. I went down to this ravine here just as I was about to spring over the bank there were two soldiers there. They picked up their guns and instead of firing they snapped their guns at me. I then ran on down east of the store. When I got opposite, the cave or cut bank I saw the soldiers horses were stationed near there so I ran on toward the river and they were shooting all around me. When I got up there I saw a young boy that was wounded. He got up and he said, say partner I wish you would take my leggings off. So I sat down with him and took his legging off the leg that was shot. From there we started on the best we could down towards the river. We came along pretty near to the bank, and there was shooting all around us that had a tendency to weaken our legs because we both fell over again. When we got down in the river I came up the river and I got upon the flat. While I was going through the flat there they shot at me again just as soon they did the first time I spoke of. They didn't hurt me anywhere.

LOUISE WEASEL BEAR

JACKSON HE CROW

MRS. MOUSSEAU
Medicine Woman

MRS. MOUSSEAU (Medicine Woman)
BILL BERGEN, *Interpreter*

Mrs. Mousseau gave her testimony with considerable force and perhaps showed more feeling than any of the other survivors. She was but a young girl, and was severely wounded. Looking at her picture, you can see the bullet scar in her elbow. This poor woman went through life a cripple and was greatly handicapped by a stiff arm.

Mrs. Mousseau had hopes of the Government giving compensation to the survivors, for the wrongs that they suffered, but vain hope, Mrs. Mousseau passed away recently, depending on charity for her subsistence.

MRS. MOUSSEAU'S STORY

"These people have told the whole history of the event. The only thing I can add to that is that I was shot, and the white men were so thick here like a whole pile of maggots. One white man with a Roman nose seemed to have a whole lot to do with me. Every now and then he felt me around the waist to see if I had any knives. I threw my blanket back and showed them I didn't have anything. They took everything away from us that had a sharp point, any metal that had a sharp point, then fired on us. I had my brother with me. The smoke was awful thick. We were making our getaway. We had a child with us. The child was dead; my mother was packing it although it was dead. Right below here was where I was shot, right on this little bench here. All of those are my relatives, my nephews and I had an uncle here. All up and down here it looked as though something was sacked up and spread all over here. There was some smoke and all of the women were headed down toward the store. My right arm was broken and I can just use my left hand now. I hardly remember anything. I was quite excited. The soldiers followed us up and kept firing. My mother and I kept going until we got to the spot these people had referred to, the end of the ravine; when we got there we were charged by the Army, they came in two squads.

After my mother and I passed that place, here these men were surrounded, if we had remained there we probably would have been killed. I just went over these ridges. My arm was not cared for, I had nothing to eat, it was bleeding but I just kept on moving. We followed on down to Wounded Knee Creek. Mother and I stayed there and there was quite a snow storm that night; we didn't have any bedding. There was a shack on the old mail route over here that time, that is where we went. We stayed there two days. We didn't have anything to eat or drink and we were found in that condition by the Indian Scouts and were taken to the Agency."

BERTHA KILLS CLOSE TO LODGE
BILL BERGEN, *Interpreter*

I was 17 years old at the time of the Massacre and I was a member of the Big Foot band that was en route here. The object of coming over here was to visit relatives and to make a general visit and that is all I know anything about, I was not interested in anything else. I came over here for that purpose. Arriving here I saw the soldiers were camped here on east and we were camped on the west side below from here. The following morning some men announced we were to break camp. In the meantime while they were calling they were issuing hardtack and we were packing up ready to travel. I was standing against the wagon looking this way when the men were called to the center. I noticed that all the men gathered together in the center. I also noticed that the soldiers were all along the ridge and right in here some were loading guns. Seems as though they were taking guns on down to the center. They also came over to where I was standing and my father had a gun and they took that, came along on the edge of camp over to where they were stacking the arms. Shortly after that there was some more soldiers came over to where I was and they searched our wagon, throwing down our dishes what we had packed in the wagon and took our knives, axes and awls and anything that could be used for a weapon. Shortly after that they left starting this way. The children dropped some of the hardtack and I stooped over to pick some up and just about that time, what appeared to me was a severe hail stone just rattled right under the wagon. Right after that I started in a southeastern direction, and as I went on I could see men that were shot down by the soldiers but the smoke got so severe I couldn't see much so I went on a little way and started in a northern direction. There my mother and I and three aunts and some of the children, who were small at that time got to the head of the ravine. While we are lying there, there was an Indian scout above us. I had a younger sister pretty seriously wounded, got to asking for water. Just about that time the scout went and got some water for my sister and my mother asked him who he was and he said he was Feather On Head. The scout then came over and, of course, we were having trouble with my wounded sister. I had another little sister that had gotten away from us in this affair and she was wounded in the leg and crying. One of my aunts, this is the mother of James Big Hawk, cried and said that all her sons were killed and she didn't care to live. So we took one of the children and started back this way. There was some firing over there. One of my aunts ran back to where she was and found out they had shot and killed her. I went over there and it was my sister and her mother who was pregnant at that time. I found she was killed. I was wounded but able to go to where they were. My sister was near death and I stayed with her. When she died I straightened her out, laid her out the best way I could. We were all brought up here, loaded in the wagons in bad condition and were taken to the Agency.

EDWARD OWL KING
HENRY STANDING BEAR, *Interpreter*

In the month of December, 29th, when the sun was well up, about eight o'clock in the morning, the Indians were just taking down their tents ready to travel. At that time we were surrounded by both cavalry and infantry. Over in this direction of the flat were white men's camps. The Indian men were called and asked to get together. They took along the grown boys too. At this time, there were soldiers going around among the teepees, picking up and taking up weapons. We were again surrounded by another line of infantry, so that there was three lines of soldiers surrounding the men, not the women. How the firing started, I do not remember; all that I remember is that I was running up this ravine trying to get away. There were some ponies, women and children shot down and scattered and while running I stepped on them. This man was telling about a bunch of Indians running up the ravine and trying to find refuge in a deep place – I belonged to that crowd. It wasn't a very deep place, and that was where many of the Indians were shot and killed. I was shot too, but did not die. The soldiers came down, one of them, while we were there, so that soldier picked me up too and carried me up on the flat so when the soldiers saw these Indians coming up over the hill they shot and killed some of the Indians, just like this other Indian man was telling. There was an Indian that rescued me by taking me into a deep place. I was laying there all this while until darkness came. I was a boy, my sister and mother were killed. I was the only survivor of the family. I believed the white man broke the law by that act and think we are entitled to claim for the killing of my people, as well as property that was destroyed. We made claim for allotment for my relatives that were killed because at that time we were entitled to allotment but we didn't get any.

These people are first time giving the straight story of it. Some years ago they had a moving picture taken of this Massacre. The Indians without thinking went ahead and performed in the ways that were directed by some white people, not truthfully but just the way they wanted it presented in pictures. That tells the wrong story. There may be a book written on that but that would be an error if it was based on that picture. They all agree that the presentation of the Massacre by the picture was all wrong. These old men say that they are giving you the right truth now.

WHITE LANCE
64 Years of Age
HENRY STANDING BEAR, *Interpreter*

In listening to all the statements made here in the past two days, I find out that they were telling actual facts. I am not going to tell anything different from what they were telling. I am going to tell such events as I saw. We met the soldiers on the other side of Porcupine Butte near the home of a man. In coming towards the soldiers we saw they had two cannons erected and their guns in position to fire. We were not on the warpath, had no intentions of fighting but we came right up to where they stood. We had along with us Chief Big Foot, who was very sick. They placed him in a buggy and came on with him. Right down below here is where we camped and to the left of us is where the soldiers were camped. The following morning all the men were called together so I came to where they were. They called for guns and arms so all of us gave the guns and they were stacked up in the center. It was understood that just as soon as all the guns were stacked in the center we were to continue on to Pine Ridge Agency. Big Foot was placed right in the doorway of the tent and I stood right to his left side. I could see that there was commotion among the soldiers and I saw on looking back they had their guns in position ready to fire. There were two officers in the center; the one that was standing to the left gave a command in a loud voice then we couldn't see anything for smoke. The smoke was so dense I couldn't see anything so I didn't make a move just stood there. When it cleared up a little I was going to start to go away when I looked to my right side, I saw Big Foot lying down with blood on his forehead and his head to the right side. I never knew that they would take advantage of a sick man. That is

109

the first time I ever saw that happen. I went a little ways then. I was knocked down, I was unconscious for a little while. I was shot then and wounded and I went to this little wide cut bank and there I found that we were surrounded by soldiers. Some already wounded, some dead, but continued to fire on us. There is no reason for shooting at us twice. They had already shot at us. I stayed there all day with these young fellows, boys then, and since then I have been unable to use my left arm but I struggle along. I want to say, I am not much of a storyteller, but this I desire to say that prior to this time, there had never been an Agent that has taken the interest in us as the present Agent has done and we appreciate what he has done for us and we all thank him for it. Also, I desire to say what he has done for us is the same as wiping away our tears. I want all the survivors to always remember this man and what he has done for us. I want to thank him very sincerely for all of us. That is what I want to say about our appreciation.

HENRY JACKSON or HARRY KILLS WHITE MAN
BILL BERGEN, *Interpreter*

I am going to tell what I know from Porcupine this way. When we stopped over here at Porcupine, of course, we were behind and I didn't see what was going on ahead. After we started to move again and we came opposite to where the cannons and hitched mules to them. I saw them taking those cannons right behind us. Right down below here was where the soldiers were camped and the Indians were strung along on this side and their camp was on the furtherest end. In the evening they didn't permit us to go after water and I wanted water awful bad. The following morning I heard from where the soldiers were camped an announcement made that they wanted all the men to the center. The next I knew was the soldiers entered our teepees. My sister was sitting down on some quilts and they raised her up and searched in the quilts and elsewhere for weapons. My father was blind at that time so my brother-in-law, Wears Yellow Robe, went over to where the men were called and I went along with him. The soldier standing on the end motioned me back with his hand. So from there I went on to my camp where my mother was loading up the wagon. That is when I heard the volley or crash. My mother and I started to run out away from the camp and she was shot in the head and killed. My sister was on ahead of me and started back and got me and we ran to the head of the ravine that goes west. There was quite a number of them there and they were helping each other out of the embankment and when we got there they helped us out. I have never said anything about this. I didn't like to on account of my mother who was shot right with me and it appears that it just happened this morning; it makes me feel sad.

JOHN LITTLE FINGER
HENRY STANDING BEAR, *Interpreter*

The soldiers after surrounding us they lined the Indians up and took their weapons away from them and took them to a distance and lay them there, so they were without any arms. There was a soldier at the same time going around the camp outside where the women folks were and taking from them weapons, butcher knives, and anything that could be used as weapons, and put them in one place. Just about the taking knives and other things away from the women time the soldiers that were going around these camps folks, I noticed that a line of infantry was standing nearby and had been commanded to load their guns and at that moment they gave us to believe that they were going to do some shooting, so at that time this infantry began loading their guns I saw that there seems to commence some trouble. I stepped out and then I struck through their lines to try to get away. Just as I was working from this line, that moment, I heard a white man's voice at the other end, sound just like somebody calling like, "hey." When that sound was made, it was about the same time that the report of the guns came in one sound.

111

The soldiers commenced to shoot at that moment. When the soldiers started to shoot I ran to get away and before I could get to the deep place there was already some Indians shot and killed. A lot of them shot down and I stepped on some of them already shot down, but I kept on going until I reached the cannon this side of the store. When I reached the ravine, of course, there was a lot of Indians following up the ravine and I was with them, and on each side of this ravine soldiers were shooting down on us until we got so far we couldn't go any further as a line of soldiers got in front of us so we took refuge in a big ravine. In this ravine where we took refuge, most of them were women and children and, of course, defenseless and helpless; above them the soldiers just got near them and shot these people down. This was kept up until I heard a voice, an Indian voice, calling from some place in a very far distance, saying that these Indians were to come out of there because fighting is not to be continued, so some of these, not yet killed, left the big ravine of refuge and they went up on the flat, but I was not with them, because I was shot through in two places, one through my leg and my foot, so I crawled along until I got over where those that were ahead of me sat in a circle up there and the soldiers were surrounding them. I got up on the flat, a little distance from them and they started to shoot them again and killing them, of course, those that were not shot down tried to get away. At the moment there was a number of old men, Indians, came up over the hill and they were on horseback and had guns, but was some distance from us but when the soldiers saw them they took on a run, so that it shows that when the soldiers that were killing us, saw that the Indians were our friends and that they might make a charge on them they lost their bravery and started to run. After the soldiers left that place, these Indians on horseback came down to the place where I was and they helped me on a pony and they took me over to the Agency, and this is my own experience. This is what I remember.

112

JOHN LITTLE FINGER

MRS. ALICE DOG ARM or KILLS PLENTY

We were taken to the soldiers camp on Wounded Knee and we got there about the time the sun went down the hill in the West. We got some food from the soldiers and after eating it we finished making our camp for the night. We were strictly guarded by the soldiers all through the night.

We arose early the next morning to make further movement. While we were doing this they took all the guns away from us and then took things from our tents and bed rolls.

I saw a soldier on a bay horse riding towards us and soon after that they began to shoot us. Bullets came from all directions already killing many women, children and men. I ran and hid in a ditch with my mother and two brothers. My father came and took my older brother to care for him. Soon he came back and said that they had killed my brother. Then my mother cried and as she wanted us all to be together and die together so my father took us to a safer hiding place and then he left us and soon a man named Air Pipe came and told us that my father was killed.

We stayed there all morning till the afternoon and when it got dark we moved down the creek to an empty shack and stayed there all night. In that house was Philip Black Moon and his mother. Philip is living yet at Cherry Creek.

The next morning we left this cabin and went on down the creek and left some of the wounded people there. We didn't have any food since the day of the Massacre.

PETER STAND
WILLIAM BERGEN, *Interpreter*

I was among Big Foot's band en route here at that time. If this was a nice summer day we could point out the various places. Right at the forks of the two creeks down here, we were made to camp and on this side of there and on the flat adjoining was where the soldiers were camping. That evening

114

PETER STAND

we were given rations such as crackers, coffee, sugar, etc. Soon after dusk, it was quite dark, nearly bedtime when we heard a sort of metallic sound as though soldiers were moving and came to where the men were camping and about that time we heard some Indians right across from us talking. The women went after water, came back and reported that the infantry and the cavalry had surrounded us. We didn't know what to think, after hearing all of that, we were kind of a little bit afraid and it bothered us a little through the night until morning. I want to state that there was a tent erected right near the soldiers for Big Foot, who was troubled with a hemorrhage at that time.

The next morning, from this tent, some one announced that all men should come to that spot to talk with the officer. This announcer was stating that the large boys were to come also so we all went. We boys were placed just back of the men, out towards the creek out here to one side right in a body. About that time there was about six soldiers that came to where the men were and commenced to search them, threw their blankets back and searched them, also searched them through the legs. When they were through with them they also went over to where the women were packing up to move. I saw the soldiers come to surround us, two lines of infantry, two lines of cavalry around us. As I stated there was some commotion, I raised my arm up and they fired the volley. As the volley was flying into us, we couldn't see anything — everything was smoking from then on; this valley was just covered with smoke so I didn't see anything. Right after the volley was fired, I heard somebody bellow in Indian for them to throw themselves flat on the ground so I did as he announced.

Later I started for our camp but the smoke was so thick I couldn't see anything, the first thing I knew someone hit me, on my right side, that is I ran into someone. I straightened up and started again, and ran into somebody's leg again but didn't fall that time. I kept running until I got where the camp was. I noticed there was one of the horses was shot

116

down and the other was still alive but all tangled up so I went on by the wagon box and on up the hill laid flat on my back. From where I laid, I could see men, women and children coming. As I looked over that way I could see them shot down one after another. We were not harmed much in there because we dug a trench. There were women that dug in there, most of them with their hands. I got there too and just stayed there all day. There was lots of women and children and there was about sixty of us in this trench. Most of them were killed but four of us men, about seven women and the rest were all killed. That evening after they had ceased firing we started up that creek on foot. We saw our relatives lying dead all around there. We looked them over as we went. We got up to these pines at the head of this ravine.

DONALD BLUE HAIR
WILLIAM BERGEN, *Interpreter*

Right down here, below where you see this land, is where we, the Indians, were camped. I was with Big Foot's band. The morning after we made our camp there, all of the men were requested to come to the center then they began to search for arms, throwing our blankets back and searching us. They took everything, any kind of knife, even beading awls. After taking everything away from us that had a sharp point, we were all bunched up. Right on top of this hill, the cavalry surrounded the entire camp. The infantry surrounded us. After these soldiers that were searching for arms return, they shot the volley into us. At that time they were using black powder and the smoke was like a fog. I didn't know where they were running to but they were all running towards the store or up the ravine. From the first volley that was shot into us, they just continued to shoot. I ran around this little ridge over here then circled around and came back down into the ravine. That is where I stayed or laid all day long. There were others with me.

117

STATEMENT OF AFRAID OF THE ENEMY
May 25, 1932,

I am 78 years old, so you can judge that I know quite a lot of things which occurred. I am not going to talk about these creeks and rivers. I know that I was with Big Foot's band that was called over here. We came over here to see some of the Oglala Chiefs and just unconcerned about anything else. When we saw the soldiers coming we tied a white flag to a pole and held it so the soldiers could see it. We went into camp with them and I never thought that anything would happen. I saw some of the soldiers and Indians and some of my relations and was not afraid of anything that evening. I went over to see Big Foot in a soldiers' tent where he was sick.

The next morning the officer told Big Foot that they wanted all his guns. He was our chief and we looked to him to say something but he was coughing all the time. Finally he said you men better give him your guns, we are not on this trip to do any fighting but we came over here to see our relatives and to be at Red Cloud's council. Shortly after that the soldiers started out among the Indians searching them and they went to our tents to search for things.

We were a band of people that respected God and we did not think there was going to be any harm done. I looked over and saw an officer on a sorrel horse coming around the left end of the camp. I heard him give some command and right after the command it sounded like a lightning crash. That is about all I know. When I became conscious I was lying down. As I arose and started to go I began to get unconscious again. For that reason I do not know a great deal of what took place after this. I have my old cloak and it has nine bullet holes in it. I am shot all through the body and I may die anytime from the effects of those wounds. I was bleeding from my nose and mouth. I want my good friends to tell the good white people what they did to us here at Wounded Knee. We know he is our friend and we know that some white people

118

are good friends of the Indians, but most of them do not like us and not have sympathy for us poor Indians. The missionaries have been good friends to the Indians and love them. We don't have hate in our hearts for the white people, but the soldiers tried to murder us and we want the Government to find out the truth, not like the picture show that came here and had the Indians to act just like they wanted but not the truth.

Mrs. Rough Feather gave her statement only recently and although she was present at the survivors meeting at Wounded Creek in 1933, she did not speak but her husband did, so she said she thought that was enough, as "the Government don't pay any attention to what an Indian says anyway, but listens to a crooked white man any time."

This good old Indian lady is the only living woman that was in the battle of the Little Big Horn and the Wounded Knee Massacre. Her husband recently died and she lives at home with a married daughter. A picture of Mrs. Rough Feather is given.

MRS. ROUGH FEATHER
BEN AMERICAN HORSE, *Interpreter*

I started from Cherry Creek with Big Foot's band. We were going to Pine Ridge to visit relatives. I am now 73 years old but I remember lots of things that happened. I was a widow and was with my parents. The soldiers met us near the Porcupine Butte, and after they talked to Big Foot we went on to Wounded Knee Creek, where the soldiers were camped and we camped there too. The next morning we were getting ready to break camp when the Indian men were ordered by the soldiers to come to the center of the camp and bring all their guns. After they did this, the soldiers came to where the Indian women were and searched the tents and the wagons for arms. They made us give up axes, crowbars, knives, awls, etc. About this time an awful noise was heard and I was paralyzed for a time. Then my head cleared and I saw nearly

119

all the people on the ground bleeding. I could move some now, so I ran to a cut bank and lay down there. I saw some of the other Indians running up the coulee so I ran with them, but the soldiers kept shooting at us and the bullets flew all around us, and a bullet went between my legs but I was not hit one time. My father, my mother, my grandmother, my older brother and my younger brother were all killed. My son who was two years old was shot in the mouth that later caused his death.

We had ten horses, harness, wagon, tent, buffalo robes, and I had a good Navajo blanket. All this property was lost or taken by the Government or other people. I had a hard time in my life and you can see that I am having a hard time now. It is cold weather and this is an old house and I suffer from cold. It is hard to get wood as we have to go a long way to get it.

I was in Montana, where they had a big battle with Custer, and the Indians won and then lots of soldiers came and we escaped to Canada. I was only about ten years old then and don't know much about that, but remember hearing lots of guns and hearing lots of war-hoops. After a while we went to Standing Rock Reservation for four years, then I went to Rosebud for a short time and then to Cherry Creek, where Big Foot was camping.

Rough Feather, whom I married two years after the Massacre, was there too, and he gave his statement at the meeting you had at Wounded Knee. He saw lots of wounded Indians; so he got a team and a wagon and picked up some of his wounded relatives and took them to Pine Ridge and put them in the church that they were using for a hospital. Is the Government going to pay us for what they did to us?

FRANK SITS POOR
HENRY STANDING BEAR, *Interpreter*

I was just a child when our band was in the Massacre but I remember very little about it. I remember that I was with Big

Foot's band en route here and that we camped here and the following day we had the Massacre. As I remember it, I was sitting in a teepee and all at once it sounded to me like a crash of lightning as though wire was falling over the teepee and I do not remember just how I came out of the teepee, but I had noticed that there was a soldier with a gun on his shoulder. I went close to him and he pointed the gun at me. I couldn't say whether he shot at me or didn't but I heard the report of a gun. As I started up this hill I overtook an old woman that was ahead of me. As I went past her she got hold of my hand but I jerked away from her and went right on past her.

RICHARD AFRAID OF HAWK
WILLIAM BERGEN, *Interpreter*

Those people who were in the Massacre that were killed were all camped below the foot-hill here and I was among them. In the morning I heard some man, taking the part of a harangue, announcing that all men should come to the center to hold a meeting to talk over matters and after that they were to all go into the Agency. Those were the very words I heard. So we men all come to the meeting that is where they wanted us to meet, and some of the men that didn't come at once, they still were among the camps or teepees. The soldiers went down there and told them to come in, they have rushed or forced them into the meeting. Just as soon as all the men were gathered in the center, in fact, just as the last man came in, just as sudden, the infantry surrounded us. When they surrounded us, some mix-blood or interpreter stated that all the Indians should take their arms to the center. So all those that listened to the man that announced this went and put their arms where they were told to. The soldiers saw that some of those were not placing their arms where they were told to so they went among the Indians, threw back their blankets, took their guns and even their knives, axes away from the women. Shortly after all the weapons were gathered down where the infantry surrounded

121

us and the cavalry surrounded the teepees right in between and we noticed some of the officers walk back and surround us. At the time one of the two heavy guns or cannon were stationed up on this hill, and this officer was walking back and forth where we were surrounded. At the time one of these men that was riding back and forth after giving these commands, we couldn't understand what he said, but something was said in a loud command and then all at once all the guns were fired.

That is all that I can remember, that all the guns were fired and for quite awhile after I couldn't remember anything. As I said, for a time I didn't know what happened. When I came to my senses, people were all lying about where formerly they were all sitting or standing. It appeared that they were all dead. I started then for the creek intending to go down into the creek but as I got down to the creek I saw a company of soldiers so I went back and came to an empty wagon that was standing there and I sat down in that. While I was sitting there it seemed as though all these shots were aimed at this wagon box so I jumped up and started across the flat as fast as I could. I noticed that where the road goes up the hill I didn't see any soldiers so I started for that and got away through there.

JOSEPH BLACK HAIR
WILLIAM BERGEN, *Interpreter*

I, the man that stand here, am a God fearing man. Therefore all things that I at this time speak of will be voiced by me in accordance with His command to me. Later when He judges the truth and that which is not the truth, I do not want Him to judge me for anything that may be untrue I fear this.

I am one of the survivors of the Wounded Knee Massacre, I did not at that time see everything that occurred, but I did see with my own eyes and know part of that which did occur. No one could have stood there unconcerned and realized everything that happened when the soldiers started in to shoot us. Therefore I want to say: "Anyone, Indian or otherwise, that was not among the group in the center who were encircled by the soldiers, cannot tell the actual truth of what really happened. It is true that the soldiers have to make reports of their actions, but their reports must be in their favor and recorded as such, they are required to carry on warfare under certain laws and regulations and they know that they must not go beyond these laws and regulations and have to give an account of their actions, therefore their reports must show that they were right and could not be blamed in no way, so they make reports without opposition in their favor. Indians and others who have heard the reports of the soldiers as above stated retold it in the same manner as reported by the soldiers.

While with the survivors it is entirely different, they are not compelled to make a report, nor to following any legal instruction so they have not on record anywhere an account of what really happened, no one defended them, but were blamed for all that occurred. We have not said anything for the reason that what we might say would not be regarded as the truth, the United States Government never did investigate this affair to find out the real truth and have so recorded it to this day.

My reason for bringing this up is as follows: "It is our understanding that the reports of the soldiers state that we the Indians that participated in this affair fired the first shot, and caused injury, this is understood in this country as such to this day, it is further stated that for the reasons given we were fired upon. It is said: "That while they were disarming us an Indian with a blanket wrapped about him stood at the end, when they came near him he all at once pulled out from under his blanket a gun which he kept concealed and with it killed a soldier, for this reason they fired on those that were gathered in the center. This is the report made by the soldiers and is known and repeated by others over this country."

123

Thus it is very wrong, on the contrary, anything and everything that could be used as a weapon were taken from us, even the awls that women used to bead with were taken, what else could we have to defend ourselves with? They even unpacked the packs of the women and looked for weapons. "They fought us, that is the reason we done that to them," is what they reported. On the contrary they encircled us like a band of sheep, the older ones were sitting down on the ground in groups smoking, we didn't think that they would ever do what they did to us, it was all unexpected.

Our relatives that were killed were all believers in God, and nearly all belonged to some church, these records are still in some of the churches they belonged to, some of the older men also were at one time U.S. Government scouts, I want this affair to be righted, hereafter if you desire any survivors to make a statement of the facts he or she knows let them take a sworn oath before God that they are telling the truth.

Now, I will raise my hand to God and swear that what I am telling is what I saw and what they actually done to us.

DOG CHIEF (Manderson, S.D.)
WILLIAM BERGEN, *Interpreter*

I am just speaking for myself, but I believe that you want the straight story of this and that as it happened, and I think that there are some older men that were present at the time that could give a better account of this Massacre.

I was a member of that band and when we were near Porcupine Creek when we saw soldiers and this made us all take notice at once. Some of us on horseback were back at that time and we saw a gathering in front and then we went as fast as we could to the front as they might need our help. The soldiers just came on like they were going to run over us and then they spread out like they were going to fire on us but they did not. Our Chief told us not to make any attempt to fight but to hold up a white flag as he said that was the way the Palefaces had of saying that they were for peace.

Well we had the white flag but the soldiers did not but took the cannon off from the mules and was working at them like they was going to fight.

The Chief and the Army officer had some talks and then we all were told that we were going to where there were more soldiers on the Wounded Knee Creek, and so the soldiers led us into the camp and gave us some little rations and we were told that we must camp and not get away from the Indian camp, so we stayed there all night. That night I heard a noise and I learned that they had sent for more soldiers and they arrived during the night.

The next morning the Indians and soldiers all got up and had some little eats and the women were getting ready to move as we were told that we were going into Pine Ridge, and that made us happy, as that was where we were going anyway as Big Foot wanted to be at a Council that Red Cloud had called. About that time all the men were told to go to Big Foot's camp and they would have a talk and then go to the Agency. Big Foot was sick and he had a comforter or blanket around him and he looked very sick, but he still was Chief and the Army officer told him that he must have the Indians bring their guns to the center and give them up. We did not like this but Big Foot told us to do what the soldiers say so the guns were piled in the center. I noticed that the soldiers were moving around and they were strung around the camp. Then I saw the sergeant take some soldiers and go to where the women were getting packed up to go to Pine Ridge. They would go right into the tents and come out with bundles and tear them open. They kept this up for some time and returned to the center where we had piled the guns and they brought our axes, knives, and tent stakes and piled them near the guns. I heard one of the white men say something but as I don't understand white man's talk, I do not know what he said. Right after that there was an awful roar as it seemed all guns fired at one time. That is all I know as I was lying on the ground when I regained my mind. I raised up my head and the awful firing was going on. All the men lying around me were killed or wounded. I tried to get up and when I did, I ran toward this ravine down towards the store and down into quite a coulee and there I saw women and children, some of them wounded and bleeding, even the small children were bleeding. Then some soldiers came and saw us and began to shoot us again so we ran up the ravine. We were being killed as we moved up toward the head of the valley. We went as fast as we could. Two boys were with me, one is Little Finger and the other one is Red Shell, but he is dead but Little Finger is living and is with us today. After a while some Indians on horseback came to the top of the hill, not very far from where we were hiding and these Indians had guns and were our friends that had come out to fight from Pine Ridge. When the soldiers saw them they quit killing us and went back to where there were more soldiers. The Indians that were on horseback took all of us that was able to ride on behind them and we got away from the soldiers.

JAMES HIGH HAWK
WILLIAM BERGEN, *Interpreter*

My cousin just narrated what she knew and she said that there were some small children playing around and I was one of them that she told about. I had a little brother that was nursing then, an infant, and one brother a little bit larger and I was a little bit larger than he was. He was four years old at the time.

The only thing that I want to tell here is that I was wounded twice right over there, shot twice, have two wounds. My mother was wounded though she kept trying to take care of her little family, then they came again and shot her and also my infant brother. He lived sometime but had a bad wound and suffered and then died. I have an older brother also that was in this Massacre. He is not here but he took care of me when I was wounded and after they shot our mother. He took me toward the ravine where some of the Indians were hiding from the blood thirsty soldiers.

I just want to say that this Massacre was awful wrong to us Indians. Did not our forefathers and the United States Government say in that most sacred treaty of April 29, 1868, wherein both parties agreed to cease from all warfare — to be accurate about it, it is Article One of the Treaty, says: "From this day forth in all wars between the parties to this agreement, shall cease forever." This Massacre is absolutely a grave injustice and disgraceful, cowardly and treacherous killing ever staged by the United States Army. Then the white people say the Indians are treacherous, but we are not, we love our families and we do not bother the white people, but they came here, killed us — women and children, we have the wounds to prove what they done. This act was not war, in my opinion, it was just cold-blooded murder. We suffered from those wounds and we suffered more because of the loss of our mothers and brothers and sisters.

CHARLEY BLUE ARM (Cherry Creek, S.D.)
WILLIAM BERGEN, Interpreter

To start with I want to say that I was among those that were with Big Foot. We were over here at the Porcupine Butte when we saw soldiers. We had no intention of carrying on any warfare so we stuck up a white flag tied to a stick. From there we moved on to right below this hill and camped along the creek and there the soldiers were camped right down below the hill here. The next morning the Indians were told to gather at Big Foot's tent for a meeting, so the men started over to the center and I was among them. When we got there it was not a meeting but just to tell us to give up our guns. I saw all those that had guns give them up and those that did not have guns were sent back to their tents to get them. I saw more Indians come with some guns and piled them up with the rest. After this the soldiers went among the

127

Indians, threw back their blankets looked at their belts to see if they had any knives or other things that could be used to fight with and they took away anything that they did not want the Indians to have. Over where the Indian women were packing and getting ready to move on to Pine Ridge, I saw more soldiers hunting the bed rolls and blankets and they took the axes, knives and hammers and started like they were going to put them in a pile with the other things near Big Foot's tent.

I do not understand English but was told that one of the officers gave a command. I did not hear a gun before the big crash came from the soldiers. After that I saw many Indians lying dead around the truce flag or white flag that our Chief kept flying all the time, so that the soldiers would know that we were at peace. The truce flag was shot down too. After that I started to the creek and on the way I saw a great number of men, women and children dead or wounded and bleeding. I went on past them down into the creek as I saw a few others running there to get protection.

At the time I was running to get in the creek, two cannons on the hill, near where the front door of the church now is, were firing at the Indians that were trying to escape, and the bullets hit the dirt all around us and, of course, that made us run faster, for we knew that they were trying to kill all of us. When we got a little ways up the creek where the bullets could not reach us we laid down as we were all tired out and frightened and besides we were worried about our relatives. We had to stay hid all day till the sun went down, and then the soldiers seemed to be away and we went out to hunt for our people. We knew that the women and children if not killed were hiding around somewhere and, of course, we did not want to slip away and leave them even if the soldiers might shoot at us as we hunted our wives and children.

SYLVA LOOKING ELK

MRS. ROUGH FEATHER

STATEMENT OF NELLIE KNIFE

I will just tell about the Massacre. When we camped with the soldiers we did not think of war or fighting. The soldiers gave us some eats and we needed them very much.

When we got up the next morning, the soldiers were still guarding us. We were going to Pine Ridge to see our relations and Big Foot was to be in a Big Council. While I was packing, a soldier from headquarters told the men and the large boys to go to Big Foot's tent, and while they were away soldiers came to where the women were and took axes, knives and other things that the Indian women had. I kept on packing and all at once I heard an awful noise. As the shots were fired the women and children ran for a safe place to hide. I ran toward the flat and as I ran I saw many people were already killed. I was running with a young girl named Brown Ear Horse, but she got shot so I went on and left her. I saw a woman, she was the wife of One Skunk, she was shot and she screamed and cried, but I could not help her as the bullets were flying thick and I wanted to get to a safe place. I saw a woman named Red Stone and she was on a horse and a small boy was near her and I put the boy on the horse with her and we kept going to a place to hide, and after the firing stopped and the soldiers went away I returned to see if I could find any of my people. My mother-in-law, my sister-in-law and many brothers were dead and my father-in-law, Little Bull, was alive but his leg was broken.

One of the survivors living on the Standing Rock Reservation could not be present at the survivors' meeting at Wounded Knee, but hearing of the meeting from her relatives, voluntarily sent her sworn statement which is given below:

AFFIDAVIT

STATE OF SOUTH DAKOTA,
CORSON COUNTY;

ss.

Before me, E.Y. Berry, a Notary Public, in and for the county and State aforesaid, personally appeared Annie Iron Lavatta, or Hakiktawin, who, being first duly sworn (affirmed), deposes and says that on or about the 27th day of December, 1890, after sun rise, the U.S. Army came and called all the men folks to the front and after the men came to the front some of the U.S. Soldiers went and searched the teepees, and take what weapons such as guns, ammunitions, even awls, needles, knives, and when they were through searching the teepees, all the weapons were taken to where the men folks were and set it in the center of the circle and first thing I remember the U.S, Army started to shoot into the men folks when they were all disarmed of their weapons, and most of them were killed and those were not killed were wounded even the women, and children, were killed and wounded.

I, Annie Iron Lavatta, or Hakiktawin, I was running away from the place and followed those were running away, with my grandfather, and grandmother, and brother, were killed as we crossed the ravine or creek, going up the grade, and then I was shot on the right hip clear through and on my right wrist where I did not go any further as I was not able to walk, and after the soldier picked me up where a little girl came to me and crawled into the blanket.

(Signed)
ANNIE IRON LAVATTA, HAKIKTAWIN.

Subscribed and sworn to before me this 20th day of January, 1934.

E. Y. BERRY.

Notary Public in and for the County of Corson; and the State of South Dakota.

My commission expires November 25, 1935.